The Circle of Guilt

The Circle
of Guilt

Fredric Wertham

University Press of Mississippi   Jackson

www.upress.state.ms.us

The University Press of Mississippi is a member of the Association of American University Presses.

First published in 1956 by Rinehart & Company, Inc.

Library of Congress Cataloging-in-Publication Data

Library of Congress Cataloging-in-Publication Data

Wertham, Fredric, 1895–1981.
  The circle of guilt / Fredric Wertham.
    p. cm.
  Originally published: New York : Rinehart, 1956.
  ISBN-13: 978-1-57806-983-5 (pbk. : alk. paper)
  ISBN-10: 1-57806-983-1 (pbk. : alk. paper) 1. Santana, Frank, 1937– .
2. Murderers—New York (State)—New York—Biography. 3. Puerto Rican
youth—New York (State)—New York—Biography. 4. Gang members—New York
(State)—New York—Biography. 5. Murder in mass media—Case studies. 6. Mass
media and criminal justice—New York (State)—New York—Case studies. I. Title.
  HV6248.S33 2007
  362.7340973'090511—dc22

                                                              2006051450

British Library Cataloging-in-Publication Data available

Contents

Introduction

This book profiles seventeen-year-old Frank Santana, who until the summer of 1955 had been a more-or-less unknown teenager living in New York City. That May, his anonymity was shattered when he was charged with the murder of another teenager, in an incident that scandalized the city and sent shockwaves across the nation. Santana had the added misfortune of being a Puerto Rican immigrant at a time when most white New Yorkers despised Puerto Rican immigrants—even though legally they had been American citizens since 1917. Worse yet, the fifteen-year-old victim, William Blankenship, Jr., was not only white but apparently a complete stranger chosen randomly by Santana's street gang, the Navajos. For Americans in the postwar era, here was the latest and strongest sign yet that this generation of youth was more dangerous, more capable than its forbears of unpredictable violence. Decades before the phrase "drive-by shooting" entered the national lexicon, "strangers on bicycles" had gunned down an innocent boy for mere kicks.[1]

Throughout May and June of that year, the *New York Times* told and retold the sequence of events in much the same way.[2] On the last Saturday night of April, Blankenship and three friends were walking to a movie theater in the East Bronx. As the party passed a vacant lot, they suddenly were surrounded by "about fifteen teenagers riding bicycles and wearing colorful bandanas around their heads." These boys, Santana among them, belonged to a Puerto Rican youth gang called the Navajos. A local resident reported hearing the Navajos shout the question "do you live around here?" repeatedly. They asked Blankenship in particular if he belonged to a rival Italian gang called the Golden Guineas, which would have made him an intruder on the Navajos' "turf." Blankenship denied belonging to any gang, even after sixteen-year-old Ralph Falcon pointed a handgun at him. When Falcon began to lower his gun, Santana took it from him and fired a single, fatal shot at Blankenship while the victim held his arms up in self-defense. The scene that followed was chaos, as boys from both sides fled. The next day, police visited Santana's small tenement apartment and found the murder weapon. Santana confessed to the crime and was arrested on the charge of first-degree murder, which carried the death penalty.

In the following weeks, the case touched off an angry debate over the changing character of juvenile violence. The seven New York newspapers alone published nearly two hundred news articles and editorials in the two-month period between the time of Santana's arrest and his trial.[3] Santana was described as a "hoodlum," a "gang chief," and a "punk," words which implied that he was both adult-like and unmanly, yet also "un-American," a highly charged label at a time when suspected Communists were losing their jobs and sometimes even being imprisoned. Far more dramatic, however, was the appearance of "senseless" violence. *Time* and *Newsweek*, the national weekly magazines of record, each featured articles agonizing over "kids shooting down kids" at random.[4] Youth gangs such as the Navajos, they warned, were taking over the streets of America's cities, and they posed far greater dangers than the mobsters who had ruled the streets during Prohibition. Unlike mob hitmen, who "killed for a purpose," teenagers did so "simply for the sake of killing." The press constantly contrasted Santana with Blankenship, who seemed poised to become a symbolic victim of this new wave of youth violence. He stood as the quintessential "good boy from a good family": blonde-haired and blue-eyed, six feet tall, a starter on his high school football team, and the son of a research chemist who worked with community groups in his spare time fighting the scourge of juvenile delinquency. One article described him as "the kind of kid who would be fitted into one of those magazine family groups that illustrate the best middle-class American life." By contrast, Santana was an undersized, brown-skinned immigrant who wore a leather jacket, a ducktail haircut, and, especially highlighted in press accounts, a disinterested, even mocking expression in public. Habitually truant from school, he lived in a tenement apartment headed by a single mother, a scene far removed from the middle-class nuclear family celebrated in postwar American culture. The two boys could not have been more different. Few protested when the district attorney announced his intention to seek the death penalty, an adult punishment for an adult crime.

In some desperation, defense attorneys asked the renowned psychiatrist Fredric Wertham to examine Santana, which he agreed to do on a pro bono basis. Their sessions began on Saturday, May 14, and seem to have continued for at least two weeks.[5] This book describes their meetings, as well as

Wertham's further investigations into Santana's personal history: his family, schooling, neighborhood, friends, and leisure pursuits. Wertham discovered a tragic figure and constructed a more complicated version of the events on the night of April 30. He was denied the chance to testify, however, when Santana's defense cut short the trial mere days after it had begun on June 6. A plea bargain had been struck with the prosecution in which Santana pled guilty to the lesser charge of second-degree murder. This choice spared him the death penalty but carried a maximum sentence—handed down with a righteous speech by the judge—of twenty-five years to life in prison. The press initially portrayed this outcome as the product of mercy; Blankenship's father had asked the court to spare Santana's life, calling him "the product of our social environment and structure" and "a complete social responsibility . . . that all society should be made to share . . . for its guilt in this crime."[6] However, the prosecution had agreed to the plea bargain out of far different concerns: the murder victim was not so innocent after all. Blankenship belonged to the Red Wings, an affiliate gang of the Golden Guineas known for attacking Puerto Ricans. This revelation alone turned the press against the victim as well as the killer, but Wertham in this book clouded the circumstances further by portraying a scene of an accidental gunshot in the midst of boys from both sides, including Blankenship, pushing and shoving one another.

With literally no "smoking gun" to affix responsibility, Wertham turned to the social arrangements that set those particular boys against each other on that fateful street at that moment. He agreed with the victim's father that "society" was to blame, and had planned to explain this generic reference with more precision during the trial. Preempted by the plea bargain, Wertham chose to take his case to "a larger jury" by publishing *The Circle of Guilt* a year later. The book revealed much that had not come out in the media coverage. In the course of visiting Santana's neighborhood, Wertham encountered the bitter animosity between Italian and Puerto Rican residents of the Bronx that had shaped the boys' collective consciousness. He found abundant evidence that Santana had suffered numerous instances of individual bigotry and institutional discrimination. By the time Wertham met him, Santana had stopped attending school for months, and neither school officials nor social workers had bothered to check on him. Instead of school classes and extracurricular activities, Santana had filled his days with B-movies and comic books. Wertham's contention that narratives of fantasy violence helped shape the way Santana imagined dealing with his tormentors should strike a chord in an age when we worry about the influence of first-person shooter video games or violent song lyrics on young people who already suffer from other personal or social traumas.[7] Here Wertham carefully parses out the importance of personal, social, and cultural influences on an individual teenager, and pronounces a harsh verdict: too many adults held a vested interest in perpetuating juvenile delinquency and the deep-seated problems that caused it. Adults were to blame for the death of William Blankenship, Jr., and the destruction of the life of Frank Santana. As public anger shifted from the murderer to his victim, Wertham saw a society all too content to vent its anger at its children in a symbolic ritual, a "vicious circle," that allowed the problem of youth violence to go unexamined.

Fredric Wertham (1895–1981) was a German American psychiatrist who is best known today for his public crusade against comic books in the decade after World War II.[8] This book furthers a project begun by a recent biographer to illustrate his far broader contributions in both the struggle for racial equality and the history of psychiatry. Trained in Freudian psychiatry at the University of Wurzburg in Germany, Wertham emigrated to the United States in 1922, where he found a congenial home for ideas that strayed from Freudian orthodoxy. Wertham particularly dissented from Freud in his belief that an individual's mental state could not be explained solely by internal and interpersonal dynamics. Calling himself a "social psychiatrist," Wertham argued that an individual's social and physical environment represented indispensable components in explaining problem behaviors. Although considered unorthodox in Europe, such ideas were well established in the United States by the time of Wertham's arrival. This was particularly true of a number of child-centered services led by coalitions of lay, religious, and professional reformers. An obvious example was the juvenile court movement, based largely in Chicago, which established the nation's first juvenile court in 1899. Its key innovations were the physical separation of juvenile from adult offenders, and the principle that treatment rather than punishment should be the basis for the court's work. The juvenile court was one of many agencies to institutionalize the idea that children and adolescents were inherently different from adults, and more likely to be rehabilitated with sensitive attention from adult professionals.[9] Psychiatrists such as William Healy and G. Stanley Hall worked alongside social workers, judges, and probation officers in an interdisciplinary and case-based approach to individual delinquents strikingly similar to Wertham's method in this book. Indeed, the most famous book-length profile of an individual juvenile offender before *The Circle of Guilt* came out of the Chicago juvenile courts. Although it differed in important ways from this book, *The Jack-Roller* (1931), by Chicago sociologist (and former juvenile probation officer) Clifford Shaw, showcased the insights that could be gained from a case study. Still in print, Shaw's book is regularly held up as an example of the "social psychology" that emerged from the University of Chicago in the interwar era.[10]

A more direct influence on Wertham was Adolf Meyer, his supervisor at the Phipps Psychiatric Clinic at Johns Hopkins University, where Wertham worked in the 1920s. Meyer was a proponent of "psychobiology," a brand of clinical inquiry similar to Wertham's own that called for extensive social case histories of individual patients. He also was an early advocate of the clinical treatment of "normal" people, which found its fullest expression in the American mental health movement of the early twentieth century. Meyer was instrumental in the founding of the National Committee for Mental Hygiene in 1909, which during the 1920s helped open child guidance clinics in several major American cities.[11] The child guidance movement promoted the preventive treatment of children and youth using methods similar to those of the juvenile court; in fact, most clinics took their initial referrals from juvenile courts. Thus Wertham found ample support in the United States for his disposition to balance individual behavior with the social environment.

After moving to New York City in 1932 to take a position at Bellevue Hospital, Wertham gained public attention by serving as an expert witness in several high-profile murder cases. Wertham's first book for a nonspecialist audience, *Dark Legend* (1941), was based on one of these cases. The book chronicles the story of Gino, a seventeen-year-old immigrant from southern Italy who murdered his mother in what appeared to be an "honor killing," or an act taken to uphold the family's honor in traditional societies. Gino's father had died when he was very young; his mother's immediate response was to bring home several different men, a violation of the traditional requirement for an extended period of mourning. Wertham's case study approach allowed him to diagnose Gino as mentally ill and have him institutionalized. A second book, *The Show of Violence* (1949), examined four cases, including that of notorious serial killer Albert Fish. Thus Wertham's clinical approach to the problem of violence and its causes was well developed by the time he published *The Circle of Guilt*.

Wertham's intellectual positions complemented and often lent support to his political views, which were decidedly progressive for his time. He was a fierce opponent of racism who embraced the argument put forth most prominently in Gunnar Myrdal's massive 1944 study *An American Dilemma* that racism was psychologically damaging to African Americans. Unlike many of his white colleagues in psychiatry and psychology, who were often beholden to boards of directors of foundations or universities, Wertham took direct action. He was a driving force behind the LaFargue Clinic, which opened in a Harlem church basement in 1946. This clinic was one of the nation's first to offer free psychiatric care for African Americans and Puerto Ricans. The clinic's advocates, who included not only Wertham but also leading black intellectuals such as Paul Robeson, Richard Wright, and Ralph Ellison, had spent years raising funds (receiving none from philanthropic foundations). Wertham volunteered his services on a part-time basis. It was there that he examined a group of black schoolchildren from Delaware who formed the basis of his expert testimony in one of the cases consolidated as *Brown v. Board of Education*. The Delaware case was considered pivotal because it was the only one in which the lower court ruled against segregation, and Wertham was widely credited with engineering that particular result. It is often forgotten that the chief injury cited by the Supreme Court in the *Brown* decision was the psychological damage to the self-esteem and identity of black schoolchildren. In other words, the Court embraced the view held by Wertham, and black psychiatrists such as Kenneth Clark, that the social environment played a key role in shaping an individual's mental health.

Although his role in the *Brown* case was arguably his most important contribution to American history, Wertham remains best known for his criticism of media violence, especially of comic books.[12] Often characterized as quixotic at best, and fanatical at worst, Wertham's crusade grew out of his willingness to include the mass media as one of the key environmental influences on individuals—particularly children. The emerging mass media of television and comic books were special targets of his ire because they had unfettered access to children. In his view, comic books most egregiously abused this privilege by printing glorified and gratuitous depictions of crime, violence, sex, and drug use. Starting around 1947, Wertham began to develop and publicize his critique of comic books. He published articles in popular magazines, spoke on radio and television, and addressed several official bodies, most famously the U.S. Senate Subcommittee to Investigate Juvenile Delinquency in 1954. That same year marked the publication of

Seduction of the Innocent, and the peak of Wertham's public influence. Already he was being mocked by his colleagues in the social and behavioral sciences as an unscientific demagogue who argued without proof that children robotically identified with and imitated fictional characters. As his most recent biographer notes, however, Wertham simply wanted children to be protected from inappropriately adult scenes and situations, particularly the crudest kind that he associated with the largest culture industries.[13] He opposed all calls for censorship and viewed the formation of the Comics Code Authority as a frustrating defeat. Once we consider Wertham's extensive work with poor and nonwhite youth, it becomes obvious that he was especially concerned about children and adolescents who lived with poverty, discrimination, and absentee parents. In this book, he argues quite plausibly that for these children, media violence filled a deep void that easily could lead to destructive ends.

The comic book episode has come to define Wertham and, in the process, has obscured his substantial body of work. Upon his death in 1981, the *New York Times* published an obituary that somehow managed to omit any mention of the LaFargue Clinic or the *Brown* testimony, eliciting a reproachful letter from NAACP attorney Jack Greenberg.[14] The comic book shadow also fell over this book, the first one that Wertham published after *Seduction of the Innocent*. Only a few indifferent reviews appeared on *The Circle of Guilt*, each of them focused disproportionately on its chapter on comic books, which at ten pages is the shortest chapter in the book. Albert Deutsch, the famous critic of mental hospitals, devoted more than half of his review to "Wertham's tendency to exaggerate the comic-book evil out of all proportion."[15] A reviewer in *The Nation* called it "a superficial book" that furnished Wertham "with more ammunition for his one-man campaign against crime comics."[16] Critics acknowledged but did not credit the epic sweep of this book, which ranges from Puerto Rico to the Bronx slums. *The Circle of Guilt* combined Wertham's disparate intellectual and political concerns for social psychiatry, media violence, and racial inequality more comprehensively than any of his other published work. The end result was far more innovative and forward looking than was understood at the time.

This book is far more than a window into underappreciated facets of the career of Fredric Wertham. It serves as an index for a host of social and cultural changes that wracked the postwar era. Chief among those covered here was the jarring movement of populations from rural towns to urban centers, across state and national borders.[17] New York City was one of many American metropolises in the northeast and midwest affected by the emigration of the descendants of immigrants from southern and eastern Europe. They followed the lure of affordable suburban housing, in master-planned communities such as Levittown, where mortgage payments were often cheaper than monthly rents in urban tenements. As the so-called "white ethnics" began to leave their old neighborhoods, they were replaced by African Americans and Latinos, many of whom had come during World War II when defense jobs were more plentiful. Once the war ended, however, nonwhites often did not share equally in the postwar employment and housing booms. Residential segregation policies, often unwritten, prevented movement to the suburbs even for those who could afford it. As the 1950s progressed, jobs began to dry up, as large-scale industries began to vacate urban cores for suburban areas where land costs were cheaper. Some companies began to leave the region altogether for the south and southwest regions, where labor unions and government regulations were scarce, fueling the "sun belt" boom of later decades. By the 1970s, social scientists would speak of "deindustrialization," a phenomenon that urban historians have traced to the early postwar period and that helped shape this book's story.

However, the transition of distinct populations in urban neighborhoods, first identified as "succession" by Chicago sociologists in the 1910s and '20s, was far messier than the above description indicates. During World War II, many American cities were hotbeds of racial and ethnic conflict, as disparate populations lived in close quarters and competed for urban space and resources. One of the more visible fronts in this ongoing conflict was the street, where adolescent boys formed peer groups that sometimes served as social clubs, and other times hardened into gangs. Authorities often had trouble telling the difference, as Wertham suggests here; the Navajos began as a stickball club but transformed into a means of self-defense for Puerto Rican youth. In his seminal study of urban youth groups, the sociologist William Foote Whyte observed that youth gangs often acted with the sanction of neighborhood adults, even if they appeared "delinquent" to outsiders.[18] While this was hardly new—nineteenth-century gangs in New York often had youth auxiliaries—it took on a more autonomous character in the 1950s. Increasingly, youth gangs such as the Navajos, the Golden Guineas, and the Red Wings (not to mention the Fordham Baldies or the Egyptian Kings) were carving out and defending local "turf" on their own, with deadly results that were becoming hard to ignore.[19]

Immigrants from the Caribbean, particularly Puerto Rico, were often the targets of turf wars. Although Puerto Ricans had been immigrating to New York since the time of the Spanish-American War, they came in larger numbers after World War II. In the fifteen years following the war, an average of forty thousand migrants left the grinding poverty of Puerto Rico annually, almost all for New York City. By 1980, over a third of all Puerto Rican–born people between the ages of twenty-five and forty-four were living in the United States.[20] Like African American migrants, Puerto Ricans often found themselves moving constantly between tenements in older neighborhoods. By the time Wertham encountered him, Frank Santana had moved several times, after having relocated from Puerto Rico a few years earlier. Discrimination greeted Puerto Ricans, as well as African Americans, who had come to the "promised land" of New York City hoping to establish a higher standard of living. Instead, they found tenements overpriced by slumlords who knew these tenants could not relocate easily, thanks to overt and tacit forms of discrimination in housing. They found schools that tracked their children into a vocational rather than an academic curriculum, the era's equivalent of special education classes. Language formed an enormous barrier which many teachers showed little interest in surmounting, and which often made the lure of the city streets that much greater for disinterested and disaffected teenagers like Santana. Social service agencies were tardy and indifferent in offering assistance to these families; schoolteachers and social workers alike were too often unwilling or unable to bridge the cultural divides that would have allowed them to help more. It did not help the new immigrants that they belonged to a *criollo* or creole people descended from indigenous, African, and Spanish origins. This quality seems to have made them appear even more alien to white New Yorkers whose parents and grandparents had suffered discrimination for being "too foreign" themselves.

Wertham's methodological contention that a psychiatrist must investigate a patient's social environment will seem obvious to contemporary readers, but he was working against the grain of social thought in the 1950s. Postwar experts analyzed the long-studied problem of juvenile delinquency by narrowing its root causes to individual failures to adjust to the newly affluent society. Even urban sociologists who studied youth gangs began to portray them as separate societies or "delinquent subcultures" that operated in deliberate opposition to the middle-class mainstream.[21] Wertham found such views morally bankrupt because they shifted the responsibility for what he viewed as the real root causes—poverty, inequality, discrimination—

onto the shoulders of relatively powerless people like the Santana family. In essence, Wertham suspected a "blame-the-victim" mentality lay behind elaborate-sounding theories. He also found pathologizing responses to delinquency to be completely inadequate to halt the spread of the problem, a view that was borne out by subsequent events.

After the Santana case, street violence in the boroughs of the Bronx and Harlem escalated between Puerto Rican and Italian gangs as ethnic succession proceeded. The Italian gangs mentioned in this book, the Golden Guineas and the Red Wings, made news in the years immediately after the Santana case.[22] They became notorious for rumbles, and for assaulting Latinos unlucky enough to stray into the wrong areas. In one particularly gruesome incident, a group of Red Wings attacked and beat to death a twenty-two-year-old Cuban man who had been sitting on a park bench with his girlfriend.[23] Puerto Rican youth gangs gained infamy as well, especially after the 1959 murders committed in an East Harlem park by Salvador Agron, the so-called "Capeman," which have since entered the city's mythology. The barely kept secret about these incidents was that they could be traced back to the racial hostilities of neighborhood adults. This well-documented phenomenon received abundant confirmation in Wertham's hands, particularly in one telling discussion with a white adult from the neighborhood who is sympathetic to Santana but afraid to testify as a character witness on his behalf. The "terror" Wertham describes here echoes the atmosphere of the Deep South in the civil rights era, when blacks and whites alike who dared to oppose the Jim Crow order in even the most insignificant way were taking their lives (and those of their families) in their own hands.[24] Youth gangs enforced their community's desires to keep rival ethnic and racial groups away from their streets, public parks, swimming pools, settlement houses, and community centers, but they also were visible parts of an atmosphere of fear.[25]

The new breed of youth gang began to surface in the era's popular culture. The earliest example may have been *The Blackboard Jungle* (1954), a Hollywood film based on a novel by Evan Hunter, a former Bronx schoolteacher. This film set the standard for classroom dramas in which a white teacher attempts to reform the crumbling inner-city school and its racially and ethnically diverse student body. Although the students in this story are generally united across racial and ethnic lines against adult authority, there are occasional hints of tension. One Puerto Rican boy, Morales, is set up by his classmates to embarrass himself and the teacher during a speech exercise. In another memorable scene, the teacher lectures his students, to little avail, about how racial and ethnic slurs can lead to violence. "Colorblind" racial liberalism triumphs in the end but is mocked by the teenagers themselves, who report the teacher as a racist to the principal. At one point, a gang of students clad in identically marked leather jackets assaults two teachers in an alley. Ironically, the public reaction to the film focused mainly on its negative depiction of American schools. Youth gangs became a staple of "teenpics," a genre of films aimed at adolescent audiences that told stories from their viewpoint.[26] However, some films about youth gangs focused specifically on New York. Perhaps the most famous example is *West Side Story* (1961), a film adapted from an award-winning Broadway musical which won the Academy Award for Best Picture. Here the city's gangs, the Jets and the Sharks, are reduced to feuding Capulets and Montagues (patterned after Shakespeare's Romeo and Juliet), in a tale of forbidden love between an Italian boy and a Puerto Rican girl. That same year offered a more hard-boiled rendering, *The Young Savages* (1961), a murder mystery in which an assistant district attorney investigates the murder of a blind Puerto Rican boy by a group of Italian gang members. One of the Italian characters seems ripped from the pages of this book: Anthony "Batman" Aposto, who is mentally retarded and actually believes that he is Batman.

Both Wertham and the press dwelled too much upon the gang nicknames taken by Santana ("Tarzan") and Falcon ("Superman"), an obsession which betrayed a failure to comprehend the youth culture of the streets comprised of "bop" and rock music, ducktail haircuts, leather jackets, colors, graffiti, dances, and language. The absence of any discussion of culture is one of the only major shortcomings of *The Circle of Guilt*. Too often Wertham portrays his patient as a hapless victim who reacts in a simple and unselfconscious fashion to the events swirling around him. This was one major weakness of the postwar generation of white liberal intellectuals that Wertham seems to have shared: a tendency to view nonwhites only as sympathetic but psychologically damaged subjects who lacked meaningful agency.[27] For experts, urban youth did not even own a culture of their own worth understanding, not only because they inhabited a "deviant" environment, but due to their age. In general, adolescents were subjects for psychologists rather than autonomous beings.

Young people began to take matters into their own hands more directly in the 1960s, mounting social criticisms that in some cases can be found in these pages. Wertham's fantasy of a "delinquent strike" is stunning for its evocation of New Left indictments of a "sick society." His argument that entrenched bureaucracies sustained themselves by perpetuating a certain amount of juvenile delinquency predicts the anti-institutional critiques of Paul Goodman and Edgar Z. Friedenberg.[28] Most strikingly, his vision of racial and ethnic brotherhood very nearly forecasts the civil rights marches of the 1960s, particularly the scene at the Lincoln Memorial in March 1963, when Martin Luther King, Jr., delivered his "I Have a Dream" speech. The decade, however, belonged to young people, who stood in the front lines of a plethora of social movements, many of which were based on racial, ethnic, gender, or sexual identity.[29]

Youth also figured prominently in the expansion of individual and group rights, a trend which by the late 1960s helped spur a children's rights movement.[30] Many of this movement's major achievements came in the area of juvenile justice, as court decisions extended a host of constitutional rights to accused juveniles. It was thought at the time that the inclusion of due process rights in juvenile justice would further the project of the Progressive-era creators of the juvenile court. Too often, juveniles had been subjected to adult justice and sometimes worse, as the case of Frank Santana suggests. Legal historians, however, have argued that the inclusion of adult protections eventually gave rise to a push to subject juveniles to adult punishments—a movement that by the 1980s was expressed in the slogan "adult time for adult crime." This shift hastened the trend toward disproportionate punishment and incarceration of African American and Latino youth, surely an unanticipated outcome to the advocates of children's rights in the 1960s.

One of the beneficiaries of the rights revolution, ironically enough, was Frank Santana himself, whose adolescence was long over by the time the revolution had crested. In 1969, with an affidavit from the New York State Bar Association, he appealed his sentence successfully to the New York State Supreme Court on the grounds that his plea bargain had been struck in a hopelessly hostile atmosphere surrounding his trial. The court was moved by Santana's "extreme youth" at the time of his trial, coupled with the "exceptionally long" and "very seldom imposed" sentence. It also noted that Santana had pled guilty "solely because" he and his attorney feared he would receive a death sentence due to public anger in the Bronx at the time of his trial. Attempts to delay the trial or have it moved to a new venue had been denied, leaving Santana little choice.[31]

One wonders if he ever read this treatment of his story, and what he would think of it. Perhaps he would fault Fredric Wertham for crediting him with so little power over his own fate. One suspects, however, that the summer of 1955 is not a time that he would wish to revisit: a time of great tragedy, anger, and sadness, brought to life in this book.

Twenty-first century readers may be struck by the relevance of *The Circle of Guilt* to current affairs. Youth violence has continued to elicit great personal and public anguish in American life. Wertham's language evokes contemporary responses to increasingly theatrical teenage murders, both on the city streets and in well-endowed suburban high schools. A preoccupation with the influence of popular culture characterizes latter-day explanations even more than those offered by Wertham, whose reputation for being obsessed with media violence seems by comparison both prescient and undeserved. Perhaps the most arresting feature of this book is its willingness to tackle what are essentially political questions of social inequality. Wertham is not interested in reducing Frank Santana to a copycat criminal, or classifying him as a product of peer pressure or a generalized low self-esteem. Instead he confronts us with the tangled web of public policy, institutionalized inequality, and individual discrimination that continues to ensnare far too many teenagers.

William Bush

1. "Strangers on Bikes Slay Boy in Street," *New York Times*, May 1, 1955.

2. The following is a composite of "Strangers on Bikes;" "Hoodlum, 17, Seized As Slayer of Boy, 15," *NYT*, May 2, 1955; and Wertham's account in this book.

3. This figure comes from *New York v. Frank Santana*, 31 A.D.2d 904; 298 N.Y.S.2d 120; 1969 N.Y. App. Div. LEXIS 4411, March 13, 1969.

4. "The Problem Grows Worse . . . What to Do When Kids Shoot Down Kids?" *Newsweek*, May 16, 1955, 32–34; "Return to the Poconos," *Time*, May 16, 1955, 28–29; "Stop Glamorizing Crime," *America*, May 21, 1955, 202–3; "Juvenile Crime and the Community's Responsibility," *School and Society* 81 (June 11, 1955): 188.

5. "Visitor for Santana," *NYT*, May 14, 1955.

6. "Boy Killer Wins Second-Degree Term," *NYT*, June 9, 1955.

7. See for example "The Monsters Next Door: A Special Report on the Colorado School Massacre," *Time*, May 3, 1999, 20–54.

8. This biographical discussion draws heavily on Bart Beaty, *Fredric Wertham and the Critique of Mass Culture* (Jackson: University Press of Mississippi, 2005).

9. There is a vast literature on the history of the juvenile court. For an introduction, see most recently Steven L. Schlossman, *Transforming Juvenile Justice: Reform Ideals and Institutional*

Realities, 1825–1920 (DeKalb: Northern Illinois University Press, 2005 [1977]); and David S. Tanenhaus, *Juvenile Justice in the Making* (New York: Oxford University Press, 2004).

10. Clifford R. Shaw, *The Jack-Roller: A Delinquent Boy's Own Story* (Chicago: University of Chicago Press, 1930).

11. The above description draws on Gerald N. Grob, *From Asylum to Community: Mental Health Policy in Modern America* (Princeton: Princeton University Press, 1991); and Margo Horn, *Before It's Too Late: The Child Guidance Movement in the United States* (Philadelphia: Temple University Press, 1989).

12. Besides Beaty, *Fredric Wertham and the Critique of Mass Culture*, books that explore the anti–comic book crusade include James A. Gilbert, *A Cycle of Outrage: America's Reaction to the Juvenile Delinquent in the 1950s* (New York: Oxford University Press, 1986); Amy Kiste Nyberg, *Seal of Approval: The History of the Comics Code* (Jackson: University Press of Mississippi, 1998); and Bradford W. Wright, *Comic Book Nation: The Transformation of Youth Culture in America* (Baltimore: Johns Hopkins University Press, 2001), 86–179.

13. This is one of the main arguments of Beaty, *Fredric Wertham and the Critique of Mass Culture*.

14. "Fredric Wertham, 86, Dies; Foe of Violent TV and Comics," *New York Times*, December 1, 1981; Greenberg letter to the editor, *NYT*, December 11, 1981.

15. Albert Deutsch, "What Makes a Boy Bad?" *Saturday Review*, October 20, 1956, 25.

16. Morris Ploscowe, "The Criminal as Patient," *The Nation*, March 9, 1957.

17. The following discussion draws heavily on Kenneth T. Jackson, *Crabgrass Frontier: The Suburbanization of the United States* (New York: Oxford University Press, 1985); Arnold T. Hirsch, *Making the Second Ghetto: Race and Housing in Chicago, 1940–1960* (New York: Cambridge University Press, 1983); Suzanne Model, "The Ethnic Niche and the Structure of Opportunity: Immigrants and Minorities in New York City," in *The "Underclass" Debate: Views From History*, ed. Michael B. Katz (Princeton: Princeton University Press, 1993), 161–93; and Thomas J. Sugrue, *The Origins of the Urban Crisis: Race and Inequality in Postwar Detroit* (Princeton: Princeton University Press, 1996).

18. William Foote Whyte, *Street Corner Society* (Chicago: University of Chicago Press, 1944).

19. Eric C. Schneider, *Vampires, Dragons, and Egyptian Kings: Youth Gangs in Postwar New York* (Princeton: Princeton University Press, 1999), 51–77.

20. Philippe I. Bourgeois, *In Search of Respect: Selling Crack in El Barrio* (2d ed., Cambridge, UK, and New York: Cambridge University Press, 2003), 51; for an overview of earlier migration, see Virginia Sanchez Korrol, *From Colonia to Community: The History of Puerto Ricans in New York City* (Berkeley: University of California Press, 1994).

21. Albert K. Cohen, *Delinquent Boys: The Culture of the Gang* (Glencoe, IL: The Free Press, 1955); Richard Cloward and Lloyd Ohlin, *Delinquency and Opportunity: A Theory of Delinquent Gangs* (Chicago: University of Chicago Press, 1960).

22. Schneider, *Vampires, Dragons, and Egyptian Kings*, 91–105; "8 Seized in Bronx Gang Outbreak," *NYT*, September 17, 1956.

23. "Four Youths Held in Harlem Killing," *NYT*, June 2, 1958.

24. For a personal testimonial, see Anne Moody, *Coming of Age in Mississippi* (New York: Delta Trade Paperbacks, 2004 [1968]).

25. Schneider, *Vampires, Dragons, and Egyptian Kings*, 78–91.

26. Thomas P. Doherty, *Teenagers and Teenpics: The Juvenilization of American Films in the 1950s* (2d ed., Philadelphia: Temple University Press, 2002).

27. For discussions of the "damage thesis," see Daryl Michael Scott, *Contempt and Pity: Social Policy and the Image of the Damaged Black Psyche, 1880–1996* (Chapel Hill: University of North Carolina Press, 1997), 19–40; and, Robin D. G. Kelley, *"Yo Mama's Dysfunktional": Fighting the Culture Wars in Urban America* (Boston: Beacon Press, 1997), 18–42.

28. Paul Goodman, *Growing Up Absurd: Problems of Youth in the Organized Society* (New York: Vintage Books, 1960); Edgar Z. Friedenberg, *The Vanishing Adolescent* (Boston: Beacon Press, 1959).

29. The best overview of the 1960s is Maurice Issenberg and Michael Kazin, *America Divided: The Civil War of the 1960s* (New York: Oxford University Press, 2000).

30. The following discussion draws on Barry C. Feld, *Bad Kids: Race and the Transformation of the Juvenile Court* (New York: Oxford University Press, 1999); and Christopher P. Manfredi, *The Supreme Court and Juvenile Justice* (Lawrence: University Press of Kansas, 1998).

31. *New York v. Frank Santana.*

I   *Sidewalk Encounter*

"Believe that story false that ought not to be true."

—Sheridan

"Do you know about the murder that happened a few days ago?" the voice at the other end of the telephone asked me.

"Which one?" I answered. "In New York City there's one almost every day."

The man calling was known to me as a good writer, with a reputation for perceptive reporting of crime and delinquency. "You know the one I mean," he said. "The kid who killed the model boy. The young Puerto Rican who killed a fifteen-year-old boy right on the street. Imagine! A nice boy from a respectable family, just walking along the street on his way to a movie —and here another kid walks right up to him and shoots him. I thought there might be a story behind the story; but there isn't. He just killed that boy, for no reason. He seems to have mistaken him for a member of a rival gang. I wondered whether you could tell me something about his mental condition, and whether you had anything to do with the case."

"I've read about it," I said. "It was played up so much no one could miss it. But I have nothing to do with it. I hope I can sit this one out! But," I added, "I'd like to ask *you* a question: Why is this case so important?"

"That I can tell you. This really is murder on the sidewalks. A boy goes to a movie and is shot on the way. And then the case symbolizes our fear of the Puerto Ricans. It is all over the city and the nation and it's getting more widespread every day. I've never seen anything like it. The case reminds one of the novel 'Cry, the Beloved Country' by Alan Paton. There a Negro boy shoots the son of the man who was trying to fight segregation. And in this case the father of the murdered boy was active in the fight against juvenile delinquency."

All day long I could not get that conversation out of my mind. We remember the headlines, I thought; but how quickly we forget the victims! There had been a rash of articles and statements about violent juvenile delinquency. They all followed a formula combining great concern with basic soft-pedalling of the issues. For instance, a high official conceded the "rightful concern about delinquency," but stressed that "only 3 per cent of New York's children" became delinquent. *Only* is the revealing word here. When you discuss polio, what you emphasize is not the fact that only a small percentage of children get it!

That same evening a lawyer called me to make an appointment. He and his partner were volunteer counsel for that very seventeen-year-old boy whom I had been asked about on the telephone. He was charged in Bronx County Court with first-degree murder. The lawyer asked whether I would be willing to carry out a psychiatric examination of the boy in jail and later testify about my findings. We made an appointment.

A little later the two young lawyers came to my office. They were gravely concerned about their client. The district attorney was pressing a first-degree homicide charge, and was insisting on a swift trial. He had publicly pledged a "speedy and vigorous prosecution." The boy was facing the electric chair. Efforts to postpone the trial to gain time for a more complete defense had had no success. A number of young boys who had some knowledge of the affair were picked up, and some of them charged with delinquency or other offenses. They were therefore not readily available to the defense. Since juvenile gangs were so widespread, other boys to be used by the defense were understandably not too eager to talk. In view of some evident mitigating circumstances—the boy's youth, his poverty and the absence of base motives—the lawyers had considered having their client plead to a lesser charge. That would have meant very severe punishment, too; but it would have saved the boy from the danger of the electric chair. But the prosecuting authorities had rejected any such overtures. So they told me they would have to place great reliance on any psychiatric angle.

Knowing that the law is not too explicit on the point, I told them that since there was probably no clear case of legal insanity, it was doubtful whether the court would permit a psychiatrist to testify on the mental condition of the defendant. Of course this mental condition would be of importance to a jury, to enable them to gain a just view of such a defendant and also for the legal questions of deliberation, criminal intent, premeditation and such. I told them I had testified a number of times in detail in cases where legal insanity was not claimed, but where the mental condition of the defendant at the time of the crime, or at the time of his confession, was a legitimate issue. They assured me that they knew the law would permit psychiatric testimony in such a case as this, and that they would fortify themselves with a complete study of the law and previous court decisions.

It was decided that they would get a court order to enable me to visit the boy Frank Santana in jail, and since I wanted to spend considerable time with him I asked them to include in the interview-time requested a Sunday, when I would have more time. My fee, they explained, would be nil, since the state would not pay for the examination and the family was on relief. As a matter of fact, they hoped I would help collect some money for the family later on.

There were a number of documents I would need, I explained to them, and which they would have to subpoena. I enumerated them: the complete record from elementary and high schools—not just an abstract made now in the light of recent events, but the original school records; a health card from the school nurse; the records, if any, from the Bureau of Child Guidance, which is, so to speak, the mental hygiene department of the New York school system; any records from the Bureau of Attendance, which deals with truant children; a report from PAL (the Police Athletic League) where the boy went for sports; the records on the family in the Department of Welfare.

The attorneys had brought along some newspaper clippings carrying reports of the crime and photographs of the participants and their relatives. Later I called up the Lafargue Clinic and asked whether any of my associates there had kept clippings on the case. Fortunately they had not only kept clippings from all the newspapers, they had monitored radio and television newscasts and commentators and magazines. They even had some reports on sermons preached about the case. An inordinate amount of time and space had been given to this case, not only in the city of New York but also nationally. My associates at the Clinic had become interested in the case in connection with their research into the psychological and social aspects of violent delinquency.

Often when a murder is committed, the official versions in the printed reports leave some questions open and in doubt. In this case, however, everything was clear and definite. The news stories, the editorials, the articles, the commentators, the Sunday features, the magazines (including the best national ones), the radio and television accounts, all agreed with remarkable precision. There was such a definiteness about the official account that it immediately became established as the final truth. It stood out so glaringly against the grey of everyday life that no intermediate ground was left for doubts, qualifications, critical (or even suspended) judgment.

A big boy of seventeen asks a little boy of fifteen, during a "chance encounter on the street":

"Do you belong to a gang?"

The fifteen-year-old answers "No," and is immediately shot dead.

This became at once "the murder that shocked the city," "the case which shocked the city as few other crimes have in recent years." "New York was shocked to the core by the heartless, pointless murder," we were told. It was a "cold-blooded killing that shocked the nation," "the cold-blooded shooting of a high-school boy by a teen-age gangster, the tragedy that had a thunder-clap effect in awakening the general public." A pamphlet on juvenile delinquency began like this: "The shocking murder of fifteen-year-old William Blankenship, by a teen-age gang, focuses public attention as never before on the acute problem of juvenile delinquency, its causes and cure."

WRONG BOY SLAIN

screamed the headlines. (This was odd; which would have been the *right* boy to be slain?) Endlessly, newspapers and airwaves repeated the phrase: "the senseless murder"; "the senseless slaying"; "the senseless killing of the model boy." (Here again the word *senseless* was strange, seemingly implying that some other murders *made* sense.) The Chief District Attorney himself termed the murder "a senseless killing." This "senseless murder" flourished in the headlines, graduated to the news stories, was repeated by the best commentators on the air and appeared in Sunday sermons. No one could miss constant reminders that this was a "senseless street slaying," "the senseless gangland execution," "a cold-blooded slaying," a murder that was "wanton" and "purposeless,"—the "unprovoked slaying" "of a total stranger." *Time* magazine even supplied the exact words spoken by Bill Blankenship before he was shot, and reported them in a direct quote: When "a gang of leather-jacketed toughs swarmed around, yelling . . . young Billy said: 'I don't know what you're talking about!'" That was a graphic detail.

This went on not for a few days, but for almost two months. A few days after Santana's arrest the papers reported that "the Police Department launched its

first concentrated, around-the-clock fight against juvenile delinquency." They sent eighty-nine extra po-
licemen to one area of the Bronx, "one of the most
wretched neighborhoods in the city." The director of
a big Boys Club told the reporters, "The parents
should get together—much like vigilante groups—to
discuss the problem of juvenile delinquency and for-
mulate plans of action." Mothers called up the police
saying they were "afraid [their sons] would meet the
same fate as young Blankenship, fifteen-year-old
model student shot dead by a Bronx teen-gang
leader." When other murders, muggings and rapes
were reported—especially those committed by Puerto
Ricans or Negroes or Italians—there would be a paragraph somewhere in the story referring to Santana,
who "stopped fifteen-year-old Billy Blankenship, a
clean-cut student, belonging to no gang, and shot him
down on suspicion of being a member of a rival gang."

All this was not sensationalism—certainly not sensationalism for its own sake. It was reporting, representing, exhorting. It was all on a high plane of in-
forming the public quickly and fully, and endlessly
rubbing in the lesson—whatever it was. The case
"brought the evils of juvenile delinquency into a focus
of terrible clarity," as one editorial put it. It wasn't
even safe any more for a little boy to go to the movies:
"Any one of us may walk around a corner to find a
crime staring us in the face." That was what had happened to Billy Blankenship "walking down the street
in a comfortable New York residential neighborhood." There was "teen-age terrorism," "terror on
the street." The authorities were called upon to "make

it impossible for the gangs to terrorize the community any longer." A clergyman demanded that "our officials give us a city in which youth can walk safely." Everybody was informed (and therefore knew) what kind of a boy it was who "shot to death in cold blood" another boy, "a total stranger"; what kind of a boy the victim was; why and how it was done; what the punishment should be.

The key word, repeated over and over again, was "hoodlum." Who had committed this "senseless slaying"? A big headline in the staid *New York Times* not only gave the answer but lent authenticity and respectability to the term:

HOODLUM, 17, HELD IN SLAYING OF BOY

Here are some other sample versions from the press, radio and television: "the Santana hoodlum"; the "dirty filthy hoodlum"; the "young hoodlum from Puerto Rico." Even his mother was referred to as "the hoodlum's mother." In the wake of the Santana case a news-magazine reporting another case of violent delinquency said: "It was just one more arrogant smirking young hoodlum who knows no law." The photograph of that boy was captioned "Hoodlum . . ." and he was described as a "short, cocky Puerto Rican teenager."

What is a *hoodlum?* Webster tells us that it is a young rowdy. But currently its meaning is much more than that. *Hoodlum* is most widely used as meaning an adult racketeer or gangster who lives on violence and fraud. That is how the word has been used not only colloquially but before Senate crime hearings and in textbooks. It also has a definite connotation of being incorrigible and not "genuinely American" but belonging to a nationality or race considered inferior. A recent news story quotes this definition: "Hoodlums are traitors to the American way of life. Deport these hoodlums back to where they came from and we will have 99% less crime in the United States." To children the word *hoodlum* is long familiar from crime comic books, as this caption from a July, 1955, comic book illustrates:

Cop Kills Hoodlum after Stick-up

They have learned that the hoodlum is an un-American-looking man, legitimate prey for violence of the Superman type.

Accounts of the Santana case supplied these details about the boy: He was a "marauder"; a "gangster"; "a savage member of a youthful gang"; a "gang chief." He was "the swaggering teen-age gunman." He was also a "punk," a "street mobster," and "the young thug." There was little difference between standard-sized newspapers and the tabloids, between metropolitan newspapers and provincial ones, between the press and radio and television. They all knew also that his name was "Tarzan" and printed that, too, in screaming headlines, or referred to him by that name over the air without giving him any other name at all, or describing him as "Frank (Tarzan) Santana." It was explained that "he wanted to be called Tarzan," and that he was "known among his intimates as Tarzan." It was also pointed out that he was "short" and "swarthy."

His personality was described as "hot-headed," "always starting fights." He was "a hopeless case," "cold-blooded," "stolid," "a dull student" and a boy "known to authorities for years as incorrigible and a bad actor." He was, in short, "a wild irresponsible teen-age hoodlum." One newspaper reported that he was "a youth lacking the most elementary principles of humanity." His demeanor was variously described as "cocky and tough," "bland," "speaking with a grin," "grinning cockily," "almost bored," "sullen-faced," "swaggering lustily." He was "laughing and joking and jingling his handcuffs for the benefit of photographers." (I have been unable to find any such photograph.)

Overnight the victim got posthumous fame. He was "the model boy," the "model student" who was "known as a model boy in his neighborhood." He belonged to a respectable middle-class professional family. He had nothing to do with anything. He was just an innocent bystander, "handsome," "blond," "innocently slain," "cut down in cold blood." Press, radio and television vied with one another in praising him for never having had anything to do with juvenile gangs. He was "the boy who had never run with gangs." He was "a quiet, studious, model high school student cold-bloodedly killed in a chance encounter when he was mistaken for a member of the Golden Guineas." It was clearly a case of a "hoodlum" killing a boy with a halo.

All the media of information were equally clear

about what the punishment should be. "He now faces the electric chair"; or so it was hoped, expected and even demanded. It was pointed out that Santana would get the electric chair "due to public opinion if nothing else." With approval it was reported that the district attorney "demanded that Santana be marched to the electric chair." There was even a suggestion that since the victim had been shot "without a trial," why should Santana be entitled to a trial? And the idea was expressed that the execution be put on television so that other juveniles could see it as a warning!

I made it a point to ask as many people as I could, from all walks of life, what they thought of the Santana case. They all knew all about it—who, what, when and how. None questioned what they had heard and read; all felt that an example should be made of this boy.

A university student told me, "What difference does it make whether he is a little crazy or not? This is no case for psychiatry. It's about time something is done about these hoodlums. What he needs is a dose of electricity."

Another young man said, "Of course he must have a quirk somewhere. But he's a roughneck anyhow. They should make an example of him."

A nurse said, "Isn't it awful? The poor kid! Maybe he didn't know what he was doing." And a social worker enlightened me in her best professional manner: "I think he is beyond redemption. Don't forget, these Puerto Ricans have a mentality all their own. They are so unstable."

A well-to-do business man proud of his liberalism was greatly interested in the case: "I've read all about it, and seen it on television. You know, I believe in democracy; but sometimes democracy should be suspended." A woman interested in school affairs said, "Imagine that poor, handsome boy shot down like that. Of course everybody knows that these Puerto Ricans came here only to get on relief."

None of those I asked was indifferent. All took sides vigorously, and spoke as if it were a political issue. The facts were taken for granted. It was a good example of what people are so apt to do nowadays: Instead of thinking spontaneously, and forming their own opinions, they substitute a reflex reaction to what they are offered by the media of mass information.

Once after leaving the Bronx jail I lunched in a nearby hotel, where I ran into an old acquaintance, a psychoanalyst. I asked him about the case.

"Oh, *that* case!" was his immediate response. "That boy is the typical aggressive delinquent. He is so filled with hostility and hate that he *has* to act like that. The hostility—that is the explanation. What we need is more research on the basic structure and the intricate psychodynamics of the aggressive hostile personality. I hope the Ford Foundation will finance some of that research. But I must say, in a case like this, the death penalty is the only answer."

"Have you seen many such cases?" I asked.

"Oh, I don't see them!" was his quick answer. "I only confer with the social workers when they present their reports to me. I advise them how to handle it."

That same day I took a taxi home from the Bronx,

and heard what the taxicab driver had to say. I told
him I was a psychiatrist. "So you're one of those head
doctors," he responded. "Well, I can tell you what's
wrong with that kid. He is a hoodlum, that's all. The
chair is too good for him!"

"Why do you say that?" I enquired.

"He's a big fellow. He knew how to use a gun. He
killed that nice kid! He should be electrocuted."

II   *Contact*

"Except where characterization requires it, as in the case of hoodlums, grammar must be correct."

—From Comics Code of the publishers of Superman DC comic books

To make contact with the prisoner was not so easy as might be expected. A prisoner in jail charged with a felony is under the jurisdiction of the court. He is also under the authority of the district attorney and of course in the custody of the correction authorities. The rules of this triarchy are anything but clearly codified, so that one cannot safely predict what the rulings will be. Psychiatry may have its vague aspects; but the law is not characterized by adamantine clearness, either. On the whole, as far as psychiatry is concerned, the rights of poor people—especially juveniles —could be better protected. In one case the Court actually refused the request of defense counsel that I be permitted to examine the prisoner—at the same time allowing me to testify at some length about this prisoner from hypothetical assumptions. That was an exception, however. Usually there is no difficulty about the examination.

Shortly after our conference one of the lawyers called me to say that the Court had signed an order for me to examine Santana; but the district attorney had specified that I must carry out this examination together with a psychiatrist of his choosing. I explained to the lawyer that I could not accept this condition. A psychiatrist must establish a personal relationship with a patient whom he wants to examine. That may be subtle but it is indispensable. There are big words like *rapport* or *empathy* or *transference* to characterize the psychiatrist-patient relationship. Primarily it is a simple matter of confidence.

The lawyer felt, I think, that this was an unnecessary obstacle. I explained that while I had no idea who this psychiatrist was, there are some psychiatrists who testify regularly for the district attorney. They consider it their duty to side with him and in murder cases, in the final analysis, they function like undertakers. And I didn't consider it proper, I said, for the doctor and the undertaker to examine the same person at the same time.

If a man is charged with murder and faces the death penalty, it is hard work to get his story, at least enough indications of his inner biography and the actual social circumstances which left their impress on him. It cannot be done with pseudo-objectivity. You have to blend science with sympathy. I remember seeing a court psychiatrist at work in a clinic. He was of small stature, and when he examined a man he would sit up very straight and always start his questioning more or less in the same way:

"I'm not for you and I'm not against you. All I want is the truth." I have never known him to get a prisoner's real story.

No one can examine a patient, even about impersonal matters, if he disregards the patient's current predicament. I recall a very young pregnant girl who had been jilted by her lover. She came to New York to speak to him, but he refused to see her. So she jumped into the East River, was fished out and taken to a psychiatric hospital. There I saw an eager interne examining her. Before discussing anything else with her, he tried to determine whether she knew where she was and her general orientation. She said she was in New York City. Then he asked her: "What are the different boroughs of New York?" She burst into tears of despair: "Here I am in terrible trouble—and you ask me about Brooklyn!"

The lawyer telephoned again. The district attorney had refused my condition that I see the prisoner alone. "That shows how determined he is to send the boy to the electric chair." A hearing would have to be held in court, to establish that I would be able to see the boy alone. I would have to make an affidavit so that the proper motion could be made before the judge. It would have to explain why I wanted to see the prisoner alone, and that in the past I had always been permitted to do so. (Mind you, that is all part of our current streamlined method of combatting juvenile delinquency.) So I prepared an affidavit. It was to the effect that I had been requested by attorneys Mark Lane and Seymour Ostrow to conduct a psychiatric examination of the prisoner; that I agreed to do so; that a proper psychiatric examination requires a proper physician-patient relationship, so it would therefore be impossible to carry out a complete psychiatric examination in the presence of an opposing witness; that I have never been compelled by any court to act against my professional principles by carrying out an examination in the presence of a psychiatrist acting in the interest of an opposing party, although on numerous occasions I have examined persons confined in prison on behalf of either the defense or prosecuting authorities.

The motion was argued in court; the judge signed an order permitting me "to examine the defendant in the absence of any other person." That seemed to settle it, or so we thought. But the prosecutor objected to the court's order including a Sunday among the dates of visitation, so after the order had been signed that date was crossed out on the document, the correction being initialed by the judge. Apparently the prosecutor's idea was that on Sundays prisoners in New York City jails get so much religious edification that they should not be interrupted by people who want to help them to stay alive. We took it as another sign of the "vigorous" prosecution which the district attorney had promised the public.

When I presented my order at the jail they were very polite. The acting warden said he remembered me from the Lonely Hearts case. While waiting for the prisoner to be brought down I had a conversation with a tall burly officer. The jail, like all the other jails, was crowded. There was much to be done. New inmates were coming in all the time.

Finally, through a gate in one of the high barred walls, a boy came, escorted by a guard. He looked very young—he might have been fourteen. There was something incongruous about this child and the grim surroundings. He had a friendly expression and a certain charm. I turned to the officer to whom I had been speaking and said, "Well, he doesn't look like a dangerous criminal, does he?"

The officer's expression changed suddenly. Looking at me surlily he said, "The dirty hoodlum! Mowing down an innocent boy just like that."

We were assigned a small room next to the warden's office. There was a table and some chairs. I put my brief case down and took out some psychological testing material I had with me, and a paper pad to write on. The room was quiet and evidently nobody could hear what we were saying. There was a guard at an iron wall away from our door, but that was quite a distance from us and he was not always there—nor did he show any interest in us.

I introduced myself to the boy. He had expected me, because the lawyer had told him I would come. I couldn't get over my first impression of how young and gentle and sensitive he looked. *This* is the "hoodlum," I told myself, responsible for the "terrorism" that had aroused the city and the nation! I remembered Freud's statement that up to sixteen children were still in the formative state of their development. (Third and fourth generation psychoanalysts like to forget that, and tell receptive teachers and social workers that character is set and laid down by the time a child is three or four or five.) Actually, looking more closely, one could hardly believe that he was seventeen. That I learned later to be not without significance in his school career.

There is an old saying, *"Ars est celare artem"* (art consists in concealing the art). This is mostly said by those with little art to conceal. It is true not only of art but also of psychiatry. A psychiatrist should not try to conceal his function and pose as somebody else—a friendly counselor, or a big brother, or a general physician. I explained to the boy what I wanted to achieve. I said I wanted to help him and pointed out that of course that had limitations under the circumstances. My purpose was not to get secrets from him. In fact, if there was something he did not want to tell me, he shouldn't. He could always say, "I don't like to answer that." The main thing was not to tell me anything untrue, because that would confuse me.

"What I want to know," I said, "is what kind of a boy you were, and whatever made you act the way you did act. The lawyers thought that you were a little nervous. If you are, I want to get it clear—diagnose it, as we say. Then I can tell the court and jury and they can take it into account for leniency. That is the main reason why I want to talk with you."

It did not go over too well. He said, "Yes"; but I got the impression that he would have said yes to anything. So I tried in different ways. You cannot examine every patient in the same way. I felt that in this instance a great deal had to be said to put the patient at his ease. How does one know when one succeeds? Finally our roles became almost reversed, and he himself grew a little interested in our procedure. I can't say that he was terribly eager; but at various times I got the impression that he himself wanted to understand the plot in which he had suddenly become the chief actor.

There was one point I took great pains to make clear to him. I got his permission to use anything he told me according to my own judgment. I showed him some of the clippings reviling him as a "hoodlum" and told him that if I could do so truthfully I would like to correct that. He read the clippings slowly and attentively but he didn't show much emotion about them. It seemed to me that his interest was chiefly in his photograph.

All this time I had to keep reminding myself that I was talking to a man and not a child. He was neither timid nor assertive. The more we talked, the more I realized that a certain quiet shyness was a lifetime characteristic of his. His attitude toward me was one of resigned anticipation. It was as if he were saying, "All right. What next? I'll do it." And that, I realized, was not an attitude specific for this occasion; it was a long-standing habit.

As they often do in cases of juveniles arraigned in court, observers and newspapers had said that this boy had "no emotion." That is nearly always wrong. What emotion are you supposed to have, and how are you supposed to display it on such an overwhelming occasion? Nearly always these youths are confronted with such an enormous psychological and social reality that they cannot digest it. So they may seem to be lacking in emotion when underneath very understandable emotions are hidden.

Most of the time during our conversations the boy's forehead was deeply wrinkled. I asked him several times to smooth out these wrinkles, but he could only do it for a short time before falling back into his habitual frown. This facial expression was most characteristic. It lent a kind of partly sad thoughtfulness to the upper part of his face while the rest showed a peculiar unconcernedness. Those lines in his forehead were really a telltale clue. The struggle for the necessities of life, the fear of danger, the depression of regret, make other furrows and lines. Again and again I felt that his expression and his gestures—or rather their absence—together with what he told me, were indicative of something significant. And I became convinced that here was a disorder of the roots, an unrootedness. We sometimes use the big word *deracination*.

My main task was to examine the doer and not the deed. Often psychiatrists who examine prisoners proceed the other way around. They start from the crime as it has been presented to them and try to fit the personality of the criminals into that. I wanted to start with the boy and I told him that we could talk about the trouble later on.

To elicit facts is harder than to interpret them. This is the crux of almost all the difficulties of criminological psychiatry. The situation when testifying in court is not so different from that when the psychiatrist is alone with his scientific conscience. If asked: What was the examination? What did you say? What did he say? I would have to think back over the many hours I spent with this boy. If that were all literally repeated to a jury, with its repetitions, inflections, misunderstandings and silences, it would be difficult for them to disentangle a focus. I was once asked during cross-examination at what precise time I had arrived at the diagnosis I had given the jury. I had to say that all along I was trying to sift out what was significant and what was not. Almost every question is based on some tentative diagnosis that one has in mind. It is a continuing process of observing and discarding.

I asked him why he called himself Tarzan. (I had shown him clippings where practically without exception he was referred to as just "Tarzan" or as Frank (Tarzan) Santana.) He looked at me resignedly. "I don't," he said.

"Didn't you ever call yourself Tarzan?"

"No, never."

"Why did other people call you Tarzan, then?"

"They put me in the papers as Tarzan, but nobody calls me Tarzan," he answered. I pointed to the newspapers. "Oh, that. Sometimes I have a nickname. It is Taza."

I asked him to write it down for me and explain to me where it came from. He told me about a movie *Taza, the Son of Cochise.* "I saw that movie a year ago on Forty-second Street. Taza was a very brave Indian. Taza is very big and strong. His father was the chief of the tribe." He didn't remember the exact plot, but apparently there was some breaking of vows between the "whites and colored."

That was one of the first intimations I had of the accuracy with which this case had been reported. Even much later, after sentence had been pronounced, the papers of the whole country still referred to him as "Tarzan."

In order to understand the outline of a person's life you have to know the *dramatis personae.* I would like to know, I told him, all the persons who played a role in his life. "It's like it is in a movie," I explained. "Who are the chief people? People you liked especially and who were especially nice to you or people who were bad to you and whom you didn't like. They may play a role now or played it a long time ago. They may even be dead and you just remember them. Let's see whether we can figure out how many there are."

It was not so easy. I had to repeat and explain it.

Somewhere along the line he suddenly realized I was not just asking questions to get something on him, but that I was interested in him as a human being. Of course he would have been too inarticulate to express it like that.

"My father," he began, "my mother, José—that's my brother—and Vincent—that's my younger brother. My stepfather, he's Vincent's father. My aunt, my friends (he gave me two names) and Superman" (he referred to the fourteen-year-old leader of the Navajos). Then he added with a faint smile, "Maria. She's my girl friend."

"You were in school here for several years," I said. "Isn't there one teacher who was nice to you?" He thought for a long time, as if that was a hard question. Then he gave me one name: "He can speak Spanish."

"Apart from your own family," I asked, "who knows you best?"

That he answered right off, with—in view of his general passivity—what one could almost call eagerness, mentioning the name of a priest in the Bronx.

There was nothing spontaneous about any of his utterances. He was superficially co-operative, but he depended entirely upon questions asked. Most of the time he looked away, not conspicuously so but clearly enough. More often than not he seemed uninterested. Both from my examination and from tests I gave him later, he evidently had only a short span of attention and concentration. Often it seemed to me that he looked baffled, not on any special point, but rather as a general attitude. One thing became clear from the way he talked: he was not accustomed to communicating. I had to consider whether there was not a contradiction here, between this habit of not communicating and his belonging to a juvenile group or gang. From knowing many youths who belong to gangs, however, I have learned that they frequently are not outgoing. As a matter of fact with a gang you don't have to talk. You hang around with others and may have to say very little. You may stand around at street corners and just make cracks when a girl passes. Even at a dance boys often just stand together.

Frank Santana was born in 1937 in San Juan, Puerto Rico. His father was some sort of construction worker. Frank doesn't know many details about that and doesn't remember much about it. He does recall how his father worked moving sand from a beach. He spoke of his father with great love and it was apparent that one of the most important events of his life, if not the most important one, was his father's death when Frank was four years old. That was in 1941. "They told me I looked like my father." (This was confirmed to me by his mother.)

The time before that seemed to him like a golden age. He recalls his father and mother together and himself with both of them. He didn't fill in many details. His attitude seemed to be that that was so long ago it was no use talking about it. The image of his father is for Frank one of friendliness and peace, far removed from life as he knows it in the United States.

His mother left Puerto Rico for the United States in 1950. He followed her the next year. His older brother José is fifteen, the younger brother Vincent is seven. "My younger brother is from another man."

This man lived with the family in Puerto Rico. He came to the United States, too, but when here he didn't want to see Frank's mother any more.

Mrs. Santana worked in a factory as a garment worker. She didn't make much money, but they got along. About three years ago (he is not clear about any dates) she stopped work because she was ill. He doesn't know what was really wrong with her. He thinks it was her heart.

Frank showed great attachment to his mother. She is now in her late thirties. "I'm always thinking of my mother. I always did everything she told me until about six months ago." Since coming to New York the family had moved three times. It was all so different from what he remembers of his earliest childhood: "My father and mother were nice together. They never have a fight."

As he described it, everybody let him go his own way. His mother was the only one who corrected, punished and protected him. I got the impression—although of course he did not say it in so many words—that she is a hard-pressed woman, an impression that was corroborated when later I visited her.

"What about your brother José?"

"He's fifteen. He's much taller—six feet or something." That led us to one of the most vulnerable points in Frank's armor. He was tremendously concerned about being undersized.

"I know," he said. "I am five feet three. I weigh one hundred and twenty-seven pounds. I should weigh one hundred and thirty-eight pounds." I showed him a newspaper clipping saying that he was undernourished and told him I didn't think he showed it. "I don't eat much," he said. "Since I came from Puerto Rico I can't eat much. My mother used to give me a lot to eat. I used to say, 'I don't want so much.' I start eating and then I left. In here I do the same thing. I am never hungry. And I don't smoke. I get a headache every time I smoke." He remarked that in Puerto Rico he ate more and couldn't explain why he ate less in the United States.

"Was it the food here, or was it something in you?"

"Something in me."

He started school at six, and was never left back. The language was of course Spanish, but from the beginning some English was taught and he feels he was pretty good at it. At thirteen he was in the seventh grade. Neither in Puerto Rico nor in the eighth and ninth grades in the United States did he play hooky. "I had good marks in Junior High School. That's why I wanted to go to college."

I asked him to tell me something about his two years in Junior High School. Without hesitation he said, "In the eighth grade they were all Puerto Rican or Spanish. They all spoke Spanish to each other. In the ninth grade there were seven Puerto Ricans, about seventeen Negroes, nine white people, Jewish, Irish and Italians. They fight against each other. Almost every day we had a fight in school. Not me. I never fight. They used to bother me, but I never fight with nobody."

The newspaper clippings saying that it was well-known that he was always starting fights were laying in front of us on the table.

"You really never had any fights?"

He wrinkled his forehead even more, thinking. "Once," he said finally. "Once. That was the first time. In front of my house in the summer, nineteen fifty-four. That was with my friend. A fifteen-year-old girl said something about the shirt my friend was wearing. She said it looked like a girl's shirt. I told my friend. Then we started fighting. He was my friend. He still is my friend."

He spoke English well enough to be understood through all this, though most of the time he muffled his words and spoke in a very low tone. That fitted his general attitude of being unemphatic and unassertive.

His truancy began in high school. I asked him how it started. "I wanted to go to college, to take languages. The teacher asked me, 'What language do you want to take in high school?' I said, 'French.' She said, 'No. Take Spanish.' That is silly. I know it already. They asked me in Junior High School, 'What do you want to take in high school?' I said, 'Radio and television.' They did not give me that."

"Why?"

"I don't know. They gave me just electricity. I figured I don't want to go to school no more. I think they did not let me take television—sometime in school the teachers said, 'You Puerto Ricans go back where you belong.' They said that to the other boys, not to me. In Junior High School there were other boys and they gave them everything they wanted. They were born here or came here before I did."

He told me that to be a television technician was

still his greatest wish. He went on, "In high school
the truant officer came to my house three times. They
told me, 'When you are seventeen we'll kick you out!'
They were waiting for me to be seventeen to kick me
out. I didn't want them to kick me out. When I was
sixteen I told them I was fourteen. So they did not
kick me out. Since this trouble they looked up the old
records and found I was seventeen."

He explained that he was good with mechanical
things, such as repairing bicycles. Later, in his home,
I saw a nice lamp he had made.

"Why didn't you tell the truant officer that you
wanted to take television?"

His look at me was uncomprehending: "I don't
want to bother no one. You know how some teachers
are. When you ask them something they come yelling
at you." There was no trace of complaint in his tone of
voice. He was just describing to me the world as he
found it. "If they had let me do television I would
have gone to school every day."

There was one teacher he liked, but he could not
tell me much about him. "He was our official
teacher in the eighth grade. He is Spanish. He used to
speak Spanish to us. He is half Spanish."

I said, "Frank, pay attention to this. At any time
since you have gone to school here, has anybody ever
sat down with you—a teacher, a guidance counsellor
or somebody—and talked to you about television and
languages and yourself, as I am talking with you
now?" His answer was no. I made myself a mental
note that I wanted to tell that to the jury.

I asked him whether he ever worked after school

hours or at any other time. "My mother did not want me to work. She said I was small. She wanted me to go to school. I felt bad about being too small. I wanted to be big."

Since about 1953 he had been going to church. "I got more religious in this country. I go every Tuesday and Sunday. Tuesday I take lessons for half an hour at seven at night. Sunday I go one hour, from nine to ten. In Puerto Rico I did not go to church much. I was interested in playing baseball every day."

About three months before, at a church function, he had met a fifteen-year-old girl who became his girl friend. He had had girl friends before, and some of their pictures were in his wallet. He showed them to me. All of them were pretty. He showed me a letter from her that he carried in his pocket and asked me to read it. It was six pages long, an adolescent love letter written with the utmost sincerity and devotion and concern for him.

This was the girl described by the newspapers, the radio and later the magazines as "proudly cheering the murderer as a hero." From what he told me about her she was a very decent girl, and a very good influence on him, to the extent that she had any influence. "She speaks Spanish to me," he told me. "But she writes in English. She was born here. She does not know how to write in Spanish."

"Did you tell her that you were staying away from school?"

"No, she thought I was going to school."

His mother did not know that he was truant from school, either. But from some time in 1954 on, she noticed that he was not paying enough attention to any regular activity. "My mother tell me to do one thing and I do another." Knowing that he was preoccupied with his physique, she bought him some weights to exercise with. He did it for a while, then stopped. "I pay attention to nothing."

In autumn 1954 he started boxing at the Police Athletic League (PAL). "I started going every single day. Then I got tired of it. I get tired of everything. When somebody's interested in anything they pay attention to what they want. I didn't do that."

Referring to the spring of 1955: "My mother was fighting me every day because I was paying attention to nothing. She asked me, 'What do you want to be?' and I said, 'Nothing.' I think I am going to be nothing in my life. When I start something, then I give it up." As an example he mentioned the weights, the boxing and swimming, which he used to do every day. "I gave that up."

He thought that if he would go to work he would pay more attention to what he was doing. "I told my mother I wanted to work. I always say that. Work of any kind, instead of going to school. I like to work better. I wanted to join the air force."

We discussed whether his general attitude was different from that of other boys. "I am never cheerful," he said.

"Not with your girl friend, either?"

"No, I'm always sad."

"Why?"

"I don't know why. I'm always like that. I was born always like that. It started in Puerto Rico. I do nothing wrong to nobody, only to myself. It started when I was small."

"When do you think it began?"

"I can't tell you. It was when I was born. My mother is more cheerful than I. I am not like the others, always laughing. I am not angry with people. I'm only angry with myself. I can't explain that. I'm always thinking. I never have on my mind what I'm doing."

"Doesn't anything make you cheerful?"

"Sometimes when some guys are playing around. My small brother Vincent is cheerful. But my older brother José is always serious."

"Why?"

"I never asked him why he is serious."

A prison officer came into the room to get something. Frank seemed to pay no attention to him. I waited until he had left.

"When you stayed away from school, where did you go?" I asked him.

"Movies," was his instant reply. "I go to the movies every day. Not Saturdays and Sundays. I go every day to movies since nineteen fifty-four. In nineteen fifty-three I was behaving good." It wasn't that he played hooky in order to go to the movies. Playing hooky came first. Going to the movies was some sort of an adjustment to the world offered him.

"How did you pay for so many movies?"

"The money Mama gave me for the lunch in school. I used to go at nine when I was going to school. They allow everybody in then. It costs a quarter, twenty-five cents, and thirty-eight cents after eleven o'clock."

"What did you see?"

"They always have two long features."

"What kind of pictures did you see?"

"War pictures, gangsters, crime. Crime and gangsters is the same thing. Mystery, that's all."

"Did you like to see murders especially?"

"No. That's all they show. Each picture has two or three murders."

"What about the picture *Taza, Son of Cochise?*

"People are killed in all the pictures."

Going to the movies in this fashion, continuously, indiscriminately and at the beginning of the day, is a symptom I have often encountered, especially in young people. In its most outspoken form it is characteristic of individuals who have inadequate relationships to other people. They sit there in the movie in the dark, look and listen, and do not even enter into the obligation of being interested in what they see. It is a social activity which permits them to be unsocial. It is an undiscriminating kind of conformity. By going to the movies, which are a social institution, the boy has already conformed. Frank reacted like a socially isolated individual who for twenty-five cents can buy for himself the semblance of social behavior. It is even more than a semblance. General social approval of movies as an institution is so great that it is a reality—at least a reality to and for him.

When he went to a movie, all social pressures were left at the door. Other people go to movies for similar reasons, but they do not go so continually, day after day. It is the excess that makes it different. A college student who went to movies almost every day told me, "In the movie I'm not involved in anything. I do not have to think about what other people think about me. The other people are there to look at the movie, not at me. I don't have to meet people's expectations. I don't have to say a word. It is very similar to daydreaming."

This type of movie-going is always—especially in young people—a psychopathological phenomenon deserving our fullest attention. It is not just a matter of leisure time poorly used. It is a question of a substitute filling the gap of necessary emotional contacts. The initial contactlessness brings about a false perspective which in itself prevents establishing better emotional contacts in real life. Spending the best part of every day, the morning, without any genuine relationship to people creates an emptiness in the person himself. In an immature person such as Frank this interferes with the development of his ego and leads to the superficial indulgence in a kind of substitute ego.

Unquestionably, going to movies like that gave him some kind of support. This support, however, did not help him with any of his real needs, creating instead pseudo-needs for glamour, wealth and mastery. The danger was not alone that the movie provided him with a second life; it made up part of his real life as well. Every day it was several hours of life without contacts and without obligations.

In addition to this formal aspect of mornings-at-the-movies, there is of course the content of the films.

In many of the movies offered to Santana violence and murder are depicted as a natural part of existence. Life is cheap. If a boy like Santana sees a Western movie (on the screen or on television), he can be sure before it starts of two ingredients: there will be foul play somewhere and it will be solved by violence. The hero often murders, too. But he does it righteously. In a Western several people may be shot down and nobody even bothers to look whether they are hurt or dead. Murder movies have become increasingly brutal and sadistic. Several European countries have objected to American movies on account of their violence. The British Board of Film Censors has complained about the "gratuitous introduction of scenes of utmost brutality." Under the thin disguise of sociological documentation teen-age murders are glamorized on the screen. The recent movie "TEEN-AGE CRIME WAVE" was advertised like this:

A COOL GIRL IN A HOT CAR
THE TERRIFYING STORY OF OUR TEEN-AGERS
GONE WRONG!
STOLEN CARS!
STOLEN GUNS!
STOLEN THRILLS!

This advertisement had three pictures. One shows two men fighting. One shows two girls fighting. The third was a still photo of a youth and his girl, both with gun in hand ready to shoot it out. The Los Angeles *Times* summed up the plot like this: The juvenile tough shoots and kills at least two men, assaults a couple of others and generally wreaks havoc wherever he goes. His gun mollette is a teen-age girl who joins gleefully in his sadistic sport.

The profusion of violent images has an impact on the immature brain. Some people try to explain this away by speaking glibly of the relief of "pent-up aggression." Or they say that only the child with an inclination to violence is affected. P. M. Pickard of the Froebel Educational Institute in London answered this well when she wrote: "It may well be that the infiltration of violence to which children are becoming accustomed is not in accordance with their real wishes."

I wondered how I could tell a jury that this daily diet was an influence on the boy which they ought to take into account if they wanted to understand his behavior.

From all my conversations with the boy I got the impression that one difficulty was the poverty of his emotional relationships with others. I did not base that on his attitude toward me. Emotional rapport depends on two people, not just one. The whole situation of a psychiatric examination in jail has disturbing elements, and the reasons for the patient to be reluctant or guarded, or even withdrawn, are manifold. My conclusion was based on the way he spoke about all the *dramatis personae* in his life. I came to the preliminary diagnosis of what I call *contact deficiency*. That means that emotional contacts may not be deep, or not lasting, or not easy, not spontaneous. There may be difficulty in expressing them, a lack of realization of the needs and wishes of others to have contact with him. This condition may arise from different causes, such as neurotic disorder, ingrained emotional weakness, or early upbringing without affection. The movie-going was just one symptom of this, reinforcing the tendency in a vicious circle.

To check up on this impression and to supplement my examination, I gave Santana a series of psychological tests. Psychological tests justly occupy an important place in psychopathology. They may indicate significant points for later examination or observation. Often they have the advantage of showing a person's unguarded responses. However, they depend so much on interpretation that it would be wrong to regard them as affording more objective proof than carefully controlled clinical examination. In court cases psychological tests may be a help in outlining a person's mental condition, but to introduce them as if automatically they afforded objective proofs is unwarranted and may seriously backfire. In the interesting case described by Richard Gehman in *A Murder in Paradise* the psychiatric expert for the defense relied heavily on the Rorschach test. Under cross-examination it became obvious that the reliability of a test could not be maintained without its being closely correlated with clinical facts about what the test person says and does in ordinary situations.

Tests refer to a laboratory situation, not to a lifelike situation. An example of a simple test makes this clear. To test memory, one may ask a person to remember a number; then after other test procedures ask him to recall the original number. That is a laboratory situation, with all its advantages. It has the disadvantage that the lifelike desire or impulse to remember this number is lacking. Compare this simple test with the situation when a man leaves his room key at the hotel desk, goes out to do various errands, then tries to remember the room number when he asks for his key. The difference between the two situations is one of motivation. To some extent psychoanalysis, of course, is also a laboratory situation, rather than a lifelike one.

It is important what tests to select in a given situation. They should not be given for their own sake, as an embellishment toward objectivity. They should be carefully selected and applied in areas where something is to be decided and can be decided. Some tests refer to intellectual faculties. Others, like the Rorschach test, refer to the finer structure of the personality. Still others are more situation than personality tests. For my purposes it was important to use tests directed at some of the main problems of the case, tests which could be carried out relatively quickly, with as little reliance as possible on language, and which would not put the boy too much on guard or on the defensive.

Referring to information in the hands of the "school authorities," newspapers reported that "he was of below normal intelligence. He had an I.Q. of 65 in a school where the average is 100 and more." Surely a semiofficial statement like that deserves close scrutiny. An I.Q. below 70 is usually regarded as diagnostic for mental deficiency. If he was not normal in his intellectual endowment, that would affect his criminal responsibility and the further administrative disposition of the case. I had asked for the official school reports, as an outside supplement to my examination. I did not get them. The lawyers informed me later that I could not get them because they were in the hands of the district attorney. Of course that in itself raises a point of procedure in indigent cases where a psychiatric angle is involved. Much later I did receive the information I had wanted—after the case was settled.

From talking with the boy I did not at all get the impression that he was below normal intelligence. As for the alleged I.Q. of 65, such figures are often bandied around carelessly and with prejudice, especially in cases of Negroes and Puerto Ricans, southern Italians, Slavs and others. They relieve the authorities of the responsibility of giving children a full education and a fair opportunity to train for proper jobs. They also provide an excuse for not even trying to find out what troubles children. In the New York school system, most of these I.Q.s are based on so-called group intelligence tests. In a heterogeneous population they have very little validity. I have often found them entirely wrong.

There is such a thing as general intelligence, based on the development of the brain and therefore a biological phenomenon. We cannot measure this directly, whatever tests we use: we can do it only indirectly, by determining what a person has learned. So inevitably in testing intelligence we are testing not anything purely biological but a social manifestation. The whole matter of I.Q.s and intelligence ages has been greatly exaggerated, especially in education. Most of the problems in school have little to do with intelligence. I.Q.s themselves very often give a wrong picture, and the time is over-ripe for a Rudolf Flesch to write a book, "Why Johnny Has a Low I.Q.". Not every difference in intellectual functioning can be truly expressed in a little more or a little less—an I.Q. or a mental age that is a little higher or a little lower. A realistic appraisal of actual intellectual functioning cannot be abstract. It must take into account educational, social, temperamental and other factors.

I tested Santana's general information and gave him a Stanford Revision of the Binet intelligence test. There was no doubt that his intellectual endowment was well within normal limits. This was confirmed later by the Mosaic Test which, though primarily a personality test, is also a realistic indicator of the functioning level of intelligence.

As far as the character of his intellectual functioning in general was concerned, I got the impression that he was more manually minded and less abstractly minded. He told me about his mechanical ability—how for instance he was good at fixing bicycles. I arrived at the conclusion that he had enough native intelligence to make social and ethical judgments. Yet his actual judgments in these spheres were far from adequate.

In the Mosaic Test the subject sits at a table with a tray with raised margins in front of him. Next to the tray is placed a box with the mosaic pieces, which

are in six different shapes and six different colors. The
subject is asked to make on the tray, using these
pieces, whatever he likes. It seemed to me that Frank
took to this test, where he could use his eyes and
hands and did not have to speak. He went at it ear-
nestly and slowly.

What he made was a house, which is a frequent
and suitable response. From the details of this mosaic some definite conclusions could be drawn.* There
was a punctilious symmetry in both colors and
shapes. The house had a sure foundation and was
well constructed. It was immediately recognizable
as a house. But it had no doors, no windows, no chimney. Windows, of course, represent visual contact.
Doors are necessary for real contact. Even chimneys
represent some mode of communication with the outside. So this mosaic showed a lack of accessibility—
the same contact deficiency I had diagnosed before.
Even if one were to interpret the absent windows as
representing windows with shutters closed, one
would have to note that he *closes* the shutters.

There was very little red used, and that was well
balanced and integrated into the whole scheme.
There were no signs of overstimulation, hostility or
aggression. The mosaic showed withdrawal and retreat rather than aggressiveness. Since such a mosaic
is an unconscious expression of emotion, I considered
that absence of any sign of hidden hostility signifi-

* I have described the details of my interpretation of the
Mosaic Test in *Projective Psychology*, edited by Abt & Bel-
lak. Knopf. New York 1950.

cant. The whole production was a little primitive, indicating an emotionally immature person. It was much like the mosaics that children make.

The test also showed no signs of anxiety. The mosaic was well placed on the tray, in the center. Black —a color which used massively may indicate anxiety, fear or depression—was used only sparingly and was well integrated into the whole design. The test did not indicate anything like boldness, but it was not the product of an anxious person. It was that of a person with too little anxiety rather than too much. From the mosaic alone the clinical impression would have been schizoid personality.

When I gave him pencil and paper to carry out some drawing tests he seemed to like that, too. I asked him to draw a person (Machover test). First he drew a boy. The outstanding feature of this drawing is that although the shoulders are clearly drawn there are no arms nor hands.

In such drawings there are three extreme variations as far as hands are concerned. They may be much emphasized—big, grasping or clenched. That may indicate a prehensile, predatory, over-aggressive or even sadistic attitude. Or the arms are indicated but the hands are either hidden in the person's pockets or behind his back. That may indicate an evasion of life's problems, a timidity in social relations. In the third group the hands are entirely absent. This was true of Santana's drawing. Hands are the organs which establish contact. Their absence, therefore, means a lack of healthy psychological contact such as is symbolized, for example, by shaking hands. If the hand is not there it cannot be stretched out to the world, nor can the world offer its hand. Generally these handless drawings indicate a hopelessness, a withdrawal or retreat, a social impotence, or a feeling of vocaional uselessness and futility. This is the same contact deficiency indicated by the clinical examination and the mosaic test.

I asked him to make some more drawings, including one of a tree (Koch test). More often than not, children do not put a ground line in such drawings of persons or trees. In his drawing of a tree the ground was extensively indicated, possibly pointing to the need of a secure basis. The trouble was that the tree trunk was not in contact with all that ground on which it was supposed to be standing.

When I asked him to draw in succession a house, a tree and a person (Buck test), the way he drew the house seemed significant. There were two tiny squares in the attic, under the roof; but otherwise no windows at all. A door was indicated, but it was too much above the ground to be serviceable, and no step led up to it. This house had no chimney, either. In other words, again the contact features were deficient. This lack in different areas of expression seemed to me to be in accordance with his muffled way of speaking.

Which human figure do you think has the greatest influence on the mental attitudes of American children? This is no idle question. Reflect for a moment what your answer would be. Is it a living person? Is it President Eisenhower? Is it a religious leader? Is it one of the big movie actors, directors or producers? Is it a writer, perhaps—someone who has written many juvenile books? Or is it a sports figure like Joe DiMaggio, with his unsurpassed record of having hit safely in fifty-six consecutive games, who is the youngest player ever voted into the Baseball Hall of Fame?

The question seems difficult, yet the answer is simple and indisputable for anybody who knows modern children and what influences them in town and country. The honor goes to Superman. The image of Superman has been impressed on the juvenile mind for many years via radio, comic books and television. The Kellogg Food Company pays two million dollars annually for the Superman rights.* (The Superman comics rights were originally acquired for seven hundred and fifty dollars.) The Pacific Coast magazine *Fortnight* recently reported that when "Superman was born—a new vein of gold was opened. . . . Soon there were two types of comic books: 'funny animals' and 'straight heroes' which have split into numerous categories—crime, horror, war, love, etc."

It is conceded that Superman is first in influence on American children. There is disagreement about the nature of this influence. Superman derives from Nietzsche's superman. The essence of Superman is that he is violent—to those whom he thinks deserve it. He is permitted to commit violence under the pretense of imposing punishment. Superman is above all demo-

---

* Blakely: Comic Book Publisher Says Industry Will Clean House. *The Independent*. St. Petersburg. Florida. Nov. 11. 1954.

cratic principles. He is immortal and has powers
beyond any physical, natural or religious law. This of
course makes him a constant invitation to supersti-
tion. As George H. Pumphrey, an experienced edu-
cator, says of Superman and his like: "They live in a
senseless, joyless world of violence, fear and horror
and into this world they drag children by the scruff
of their necks."

Fifteen years ago a large religious organization
found the philosophy of Superman "objectionable."
They were visited by a representative of the publisher
and an official of the Child Study Association of
America. These emissaries told the association that
Superman affords "an emotional release" for children
and submitted a code. In that code a sharp distinction was made between "the type of hero who has
superhuman or extrahuman powers and who doesn't
kill directly" and other plain hero-killers. If somebody shoots at *him* "the bullets merely bounce off
him and back to the menace destroying him." The ordinary hero "possesses no extra-human powers" so he
has to do his killing in the old-fashioned way. As a
result of this visit, the religious organization took
Superman back again.

Superman seems to penetrate everywhere, even
past prison walls. He certainly was impressed on
Santana's mind. When I give drawing tests I usually ask the subject to draw anything or any person
in his mind. When I asked Santana to do this, he
started drawing right off. As I watched his drawing
grow I could not at first identify it. But then I saw a
cape with the large S of Superman on it and, as he

pointed out to me, part of an S (the rest concealed by the position of the figure) carefully depicted on the chest.

"What about Superman?" I asked him.

"I saw him in the comic books and on television. He's made of steel. No bullet can touch him. He's always strong. My brother pays attention to that. He always looks at television."

"Is that all?" I asked.

"He was there," he said. "He's the chief of the Navajos. He carried the gun." He was referring to the fourteen-year-old boy whose juvenile gang name was Superman and who was arrested with him. Actually, at the time of the arrests one newspaper had reported that Santana wanted to wrest the leadership of the gang from this Superman.

It is often pointed out that the child who draws identifies himself with his drawing. In this instance that was clear enough. The drawing of the great, powerful Superman had neither hands nor arms! He had another interesting feature, this Superman in the drawing. He wore spectacles, like Superman's benign alter ego, Clark Kent, the journalist. So while we through mass media have bombarded him with Superman's violent image, this boy unconsciously represented him in his most benign aspect.

I had to make a diagnosis. It is quite true that each individual is unique and different from every other. But that recognition should not be—as it so often is— used as an excuse for failure to draw scientific conclusions. We need a diagnosis for our orientation in thought and action. The paradox is this: if we pay attention just to the unique individual we fail to do him justice. Only by orienting ourselves by general criteria pertaining to groups of individuals can we arrive at valid conclusions about the single individual. Every person with pneumonia has his own physical and mental reactions. But all pneumonia cases have something in common. We must think along both lines.

A crime is never the only symptom of a mental disorder. If a person is really mentally abnormal, one must be able to determine that independent of the crime as charged. I came to the conclusion that there was definitely something wrong with Santana that needed attention, and should have received attention long before. It began before he came to the United States.

In order to arrive at a positive diagnosis, a differential diagnosis must be made. Was he perhaps just a normal average boy who either suffered from a moral defect or succumbed to social pressure? In dealing with juveniles one cannot be too careful about diagnosing a moral deficiency in them. What appears as a lack of morals is often merely a projection of our own moralistic attitude into a perfectly understandable sequence of personal and social experiences with which a child has struggled. The very striving to be "good" may get a child into trouble in a harsh world.

Social pressures in the widest sense can explain almost any kind of juvenile delinquency. But it is a kind of vulgarized Marxism to draw a too direct and too mechanical line between social conditions and the individual. No social phenomenon can be translated directly into psychological categories.

Was Santana perhaps one of these anti-social criminal types about which we hear so much? Even cursory study of the data gave no hint of that.

Or was there the further possibility that the whole trouble was intra-psychic, that an unconscious (catathymic) conflict originating in early disturbing experiences had progressed to an explosive action? There were enough details in the examinations and the projective tests to point to the injurious effects of early experiences. At the age of four, just when family relationships are the most important problems, his father had died. This loss of the father and absence of a constructive father-image was later reactivated by the circumstances in New York. He had a close attachment to his mother, who entered into a common-law marriage with another man who deserted her, leaving Frank again the oldest male member of the family. But his younger brother was bigger and became his rival, psychologically, stimulating Frank's inferiority feelings about being undersized. Freud has taught us that many people have developed severe neuroses for less cause. But again it would be a vulgarized kind of Freudism to see only the purely subjective individual side. That is nowadays often done, both in psychiatric literature and in novels and movies. Whatever a person does—the "insane killer," the rebel, the brave hero—everything finds a solution when one little episode in early life comes to light! Everything else in the history is regarded as unimportant, and put aside all too easily. Actually, such overly neat "solutions" belong to fiction, not to life. If the solution based on one forgotten incident is too pat, too simple, too clear, more likely than not it is *not* true and not complete. Life is not analytic but dynamic.

The whole picture did not fit a neurosis, although neurotic processes entered into it. There was an absence of anxiety in its various disguises just as there was no evidence of hostility. The psychological mechanism of repression played no significant role so that the keynotes of a neurosis in the strict sense did not dominate the morbid manifestation.

The clinical picture is most characteristic of a personality of a special type, the schizoid personality. The term *schizoid* was introduced by a Swiss psychiatrist, Kurt Binswanger. It denotes a type of personality which in some ways, in most attenuated form, is similar to—yet fundamentally different from—the disease of schizophrenia. It was first observed in individuals who much later developed the disease (psychosis) schizophrenia, then in those who had recovered from it, then in those normal people in whose family a case of schizophrenia occurred, and finally in individuals where there seems to be no relationship to schizophrenia at all.

Like the typical schizoid personality, Frank Santana as a child and later was always quiet, unobtrusive, self-effacing and retiring. He was not cold emotionally, but his emotional life was inward and not outgoing. This was borne out by his behavior, his tone of voice, his movements, facial expression, gestures and posture. Behind his unsmiling face was not coolness nor overwhelming depression, but an emotional preoccupation with his inner reality. Some of this had to do with his disordered sense of worth. His inferiority feelings played havoc with his self-confidence. His immaturity was actual, not imagined, and prevented him from coping with his problems. There was an emotional detachment; he avoided situations which demanded too strong an emotional involvement or aggressiveness. Even with girls he was the more passive partner. This early and chronic quietness and reserve is the most frequent manifestation of a schizoid personality.

Weakness or disorder in emotional contact has often been pointed out by psychiatrists as a schizoid sign. This influences not only feeling but also thinking and acting. One does not only have to think straight to act properly; one has to act in order to think straight. For that one needs others. Despite his superficial sociability, Santana acted in isolation. Aloofness was his way of getting along in life.

A part of any diagnosis is the question of therapy and curability. There is a tendency to distinguish sharply and mechanically between neurotic and psychopathic states. For example in a recent textbook is the bland statement that "neuroses are curable by psychotherapy . . . psychopathy is not curable." Modern experience does not bear this out. There has actually been a change in recent decades in the manifestations of minor mental abnormality. The classical neuroses have proportionally decreased. The more general character disturbances have increased. Methods of treatment have to be adjusted to this change, really to help the individual patient. The Santanas can and should be treated before they commit any crime.

The more we have learned to study character disorders, the more we have learned that constitutional, physical, social and intra-psychic factors are interwoven. A person's withdrawn temperament may be constitutionally ingrained; but it may also derive from the fact that he was starved for attention not only in childhood but later in adolescence as well. He may have become shut in because he was shut out. In such cases a great deal can be accomplished by suitable psychotherapy. With Santana, certainly nobody ever tried. Nobody ever spent even a few minutes with him.

It is wrong to say, as is sometimes done, that such personalities do not suffer. They suffer not from symptoms but from life. They do not suffer directly like the neurotic, but indirectly, through the actions of others. And in a vicious circle, they often provoke these actions themselves.

I planned to tell the jury—rules of evidence permitting—that there *was* something wrong with their defendant, and that it was amenable to treatment and would have been so long before. But what about the crime? Why was that committed? What bearing did his mental condition have on that? This raises the question whether there is a scientific study of crime and what role psychiatry can play in it.

III   *The Message of Solferino*

"When an apple is ripe and falls, what makes it fall? Is it the attraction of gravitation? or is it because its stem withers? or because the sun dries it up? or because it is heavy? or because the wind shakes it? or because the small boy standing beneath it is hungry for it?"

—Tolstoi

In the most primitive societies very little crime was committed. Crime and juvenile delinquency are the growing pains of civilization. That does not mean that they always have to exist. With the progress of science and culture we have the right to envisage a time when people will no longer commit criminal and violent acts because they do not need to and do not want to. It is easy to laugh at that as a Utopia; but there is no proof that hostility and violence are an ineradicable part of human nature. To accept that as a dogma would mean being unscientific about the present and nihilistic about the future. Progress toward a nonviolent world is a desirable goal as well as a reasonable prognosis. We have to look for and combat the hidden causes of violence, be they psychological or social. Tolstoi was a realist not only in his novels, but also in that part of his philosophy which condemned and combatted the prevailing spirit of violence. Of course a non-violent world will not happen tomorrow, and little that we read in the papers today is likely to make us over-optimistic about it.

It is remarkable how recent the scientific study of crime and delinquency is. It is less than a hundred years old. The more we have learned to regard crime and delinquency as a scientific problem to be solved by scientific methods, the more have we learned that they are an unnecessary evil. At least in principle, science can study crime. It can understand it. It can help to combat it and prevent it. That is the message of Solferino.

If one wants to select a date for the start of this

scientific inquiry, one might pick a bloody battle in one of the more senseless wars, the battle of Solferino between the Austrians and the French under Napoleon III in 1859. Solferino is a small village in Northern Italy. This battle gained significance in the history of civilization on account of the role it played in the lives of two people. One of them, the young Swiss, Henry Dunant, was present at the battle. He witnessed the terrible suffering of the wounded and conceived the idea that they should be attended to in a much larger and more intensive way than had been done before. What he saw in Solferino made an indelible impression on him and inspired him to found what is now known as the Red Cross.

The other was far from the battlefield, in his laboratory at the University of Turin. He also made an enormous contribution to the progress of civilization. From the mass graves of Solferino he obtained thirteen hundred skulls of nameless young battle victims. They served him, the famous Dr. Cesare Lombroso, as normal controls to be compared with the findings he had made on criminals. Lombroso's answer to the question about why men have the propensity to commit violent criminal acts lay in the physical constitution, in heredity, and in diseases like epilepsy. We no longer believe in his findings nor in his methods. But he was the first person with the courage to embark in a modern way on this long and tortuous scientific search. He labored for many years and assembled data on 26,888 criminals and 25,447 normal controls. He was the first to make a sharp distinction between the habitual criminal and the occasional delinquent. It was he who introduced the revolutionary idea that what is most important in the scientific study of crime is not the crime nor the punishment, but the human being who is—or, as we would now say, becomes—a criminal.

Crimes are acts forbidden by law. What a crime is therefore varies with time and place. Even murder of a man not belonging to one's own tribe was permitted in some primitive cultures. Juvenile delinquency refers to acts of juveniles forbidden by law. Their definition is even more dependent upon the *mores* of time and place, because the age-limits also vary considerably. All attempts to define juvenile delinquency in any other way are fallacious. Delinquency is a social phenomenon which cannot be forced into a psychological definition, however ingenious.

It is wrong to say, as is so often done currently, that a delinquent act is the same as a hostile act. The Children's Bureau in Washington, for instance, defined delinquency as "an act of hating." It is in this connection that the ambiguous word *aggression* plays such a confusing role. In examining a delinquent we must ask ourselves what the meaning of the crime is to him, and what its social meaning is. Delinquent acts have a different meaning at different periods of history and also for the different people who commit them. Children are not naturally hostile. Many delinquents are remarkably *un*hostile, just as Santana was. Often the cliché of the hostility-caused delinquency is a convenient substitute for careful examination. In cases where there is no clinical evidence of hostility one can find speculations about early infancy like the following in a book on murder: "The hostility, festering perhaps from the time he had been trained to the toilet, screamed for release."

The dogma of the ingrained hostility and aggression in the child which needs release rationalizes and thereby justifies violence. The Nazis taught boys from eight to twelve years old to throw hand grenades. History does not record that it helped them to get rid of their aggressions. We have so much violent juvenile delinquency today not because the children are hostile but because we have failed to give them guidance, example, protection and help.

Although Santana was to be tried in an adult court and my testimony was to be given in that setting, I felt that in essence the whole crime was closely related to the field of juvenile delinquency. I was confirmed in this attitude also by the fact that he seemed so much younger than his actual age.

Even from a purely abstract psychiatric point of view it might be questioned whether one can make a diagnosis applied to mature persons in a case where the person is so biologically and psychologically immature. Socially speaking, it was evident that this was not an adult crime, though the law had to consider it so. For example, it is senseless to speak of a boy belonging to a juvenile gang—which really is a club or a "clique"—as a "gangster"; but that is what radio, newspapers and television continued to do.

It is an ostrich attitude to deny that in recent years in the United States juvenile delinquency is committed by younger and younger children, and has become increasingly violent and brutal. Many cases do not come to the attention of the authorities at all, and consequently do not enter statistics. I have seen many such cases in my clinics. No statistics of delinquencies are made in those cases.

At the same time that juvenile delinquency is qualitatively and quantitatively increasing, there is an enormous amount of writing on the subject. Nine tenths of this writing during the past few years has had no serious scientific value. In fact it is an even worse sign of the times than the delinquency itself! The experts are confused; the children are the victims. There are all kinds of loose psychological disquisitions. They often represent what Sherlock Holmes called theorizing without data. Many of these armchair or couch experts have had no real contact at all with delinquent children.

It is no exaggeration to say that a great deal of this literature on delinquency is an orgy of words. Delinquency cannot be prevented with words, however, especially if they are all put in one sentence, as in this sample from a recent publication of the New York City Youth Board: "When one considers the cost of building and maintaining an institution such as the ———— School (and anything less adequate may actually be destructive to a sick child), where the yearly tuition per child is $4,500 and that treatment must be intensive and extend over many years for a relatively limited number of children, and when one begins to realize the enormous amount of suffering and agony that every child and his parents alike endure both before and during his treatment in such an institution, and that too many such youngsters will never have an opportunity for this total kind of therapy, then the presently experimental and embryonic field of prevention assumes even greater validity for its own existence and expansion." If you read this sentence aloud slowly you get a good idea of what's being done about delinquency.

Simple social facts may be obscured under high-sounding words, as in this example from an official publication of the American Psychiatric Association: "disturbances in the ego-organization become, through a semantically exact analysis, understandable as ego-protective dynamisms with the predictable effect of a neutralization of specific socio-psychological and sociological pressures." This is no parody of mine. These are quotations which could easily be multiplied.

Facile slogans and platitudes abound. Never mind what concrete findings anybody arrives at, he must stand ready to be contradicted and confronted with the ever-new cure-all that "It's all a matter of the home." (The crime comic-book industry has safeguarded millions of dollars of income on that phrase alone; it also has served in good stead for the narcotics pushers.) Actually, in its concrete form this statement is old. Hans Christian Andersen, the greatest storyteller of them all, who was born a hundred and fifty years ago, wrote: "Eighty percent of our criminals come from unsympathetic homes." This statement is correct enough in its context. Of course the home has a lot to do with it. But it is wrong to accuse the home as a cause in the usual abstract way, for the home is inseparable from other social circumstances to which it is itself vulnerable.

It is a question not only of pressures *in* the family but of pressures *on* the family. To accuse individual parents and to threaten them with punishment is easy. It shifts attention from social to individual influences and creates the illusion that except for these parents there are no delinquency-producing circumstances. The it's-all-up-to-the-family argument is really directed against the family. It makes it appear that the family, the home, is an entirely independent unit. Many parents try to prevent their children from becoming delinquent. But the very authorities who threaten them with punishment fail to provide the services and facilities which would make it possible for the parents to have their children protected and treated. In many cases of *present-day* delinquency, the home may be all right. The child faces the problem of rating with other children; rating with the teacher; coping with the influences from the street; warding off the temptations offered by the mass media; facing the hostility or callousness of the community which, to the child, appears to be in conflict with what is taught at home. If in our search for causes we stop at the home we go only part of the way. And if delinquency starts in the home that is the more reason to protect the home.

In other fields where children are endangered we have learned that the cliché "It's all up to the home" is not adequate. More children die at present from accidents, especially from being run over by cars, than from polio, heart disease and some other diseases combined. A hundred years ago, the home could guard the children's safety; but with the new technological advances, the modern parent cannot possibly carry this responsibility. We need traffic regulations, school buses, school zones and police to protect children from irresponsible drivers. Who will guard the child today from irresponsible adults who sell him incentives, blueprints and weapons for delinquency?

Another well-sounding slogan to account for the current violent acts of juveniles is that they are all due to war. This is not backed up by any scientific concrete study and has just obscured the issue. Wars may be a direct cause of juvenile delinquency when they lead to great loss of life and dislocate all normal social relationships extensively. This we know from scientific studies in European countries. But neither the Second World War nor the Korean War is enough to explain the current wave of juvenile violence. Moreover, after the First World War the type of brutal violence currently committed on a large scale by the youngest children was almost unknown. An interesting analogy occurred recently in France where the underprivileged suffer from an extreme housing shortage. When the famous Abbé Pierre took the matter up he was told—just as we are told—that it was all due to the war. But he proved that quite apart from the war it was the result of many years of neglect of the housing problem. How many years of neglect enter into the current picture of delinquency!

Another standard formula which says nothing is

that the question of juvenile delinquency is infinitely complex, and any serious investigator who studies concretely one aspect of it is answered at once with this formula. Several officials of public agencies, which in the Santana case to all practical purposes did not exist at all, made immediate public statements that delinquency "is a very complex problem." That reduces any attempt to take up any special point to what is so conveniently called "oversimplification." Frequently a delinquency and its causes *is* very simple, is simply remedied and could have been simply prevented.

Agnosticism is another obstacle to research in general and to the investigation of the individual case. Again and again you can read and hear that we don't know anything about the influence of bad housing or slums or neuroses or national and race prejudice on delinquency. The *Harvard Law Review,* for example, speaks of mass media as "exerting a growing but unknown influence on children." Is it really so "unknown"? In a similar vein a pamphlet published by Unesco makes the preposterous statement that "we know almost nothing about what affects the child." The moment an actual point is taken up in a commonsense way this supposedly scientific detachment comes to grief. This is illustrated by the following dialogue from the Senate Subcommittee on Juvenile Delinquency:

> *Senator:* "In your opinion, what is the effect of these western movies on children?"
> *Expert:* "No one knows anything about it."

Senator: "Well, of course, you know that little children 6, 7, 8 years old now have belts with guns. Do you think that is due to the fact that they are seeing these western movies and seeing all this shooting?"

Expert: "Oh, undoubtedly."

One adjective is very often used to bar any concrete attack on any concrete condition of juvenile delinquency. That word is *total.* We are told over and over again that we must consider the "total personality," the "total needs of the person," the "total picture"; that "delinquency can be explained only in terms of the total personality and the total environment." That is usually a way of pooh-poohing *any* one factor that they do not want to consider, be it lack of playgrounds, poverty or violent movies. They want the "total picture"—but they don't want it *too* total.

The psychiatrist testifying in court and the scientific investigator of delinquency in general are often confronted with a demand that they proceed without any preconceived principles, any general theories or any philosophical postulates. The only answer to that is that such a procedure is not only undesirable, it is also impossible. Where there are no open principles there are hidden ones. As an old saying has it, where there are no gods, there are demons. General principles and theories are necessary if we want to make clear and orderly observations and draw logical and valid conclusions.

One such principle should be that a person's thoughts and actions are determined not by his sub-

jective wishes alone, but in equal measure by his objective social position.* And just as we cannot study
an individual scientifically without knowing his inner
biographical history, so we cannot understand the
social conditions in which he lives without knowing
at least something about their development. In order
to understand the ramifications of a delinquency we
need to know not only the psychological background
but the social background. We must determine to
what extent the budding tendencies in a person, be
they constructive or destructive, are reinforced, coun-
teracted or perhaps inspired by his social milieu. Subjective analysis of the individual must be supplemented by objective analysis of the social-historical
background.

In order to brush aside as insignificant any one concrete factor that enters into a delinquency it is fashionable to say that it was not a *cause* of delinquency,
but "acted only as a trigger," it "only sparked it off."
That, of course, could also be said of a cigarette butt
and a forest fire.

Reference to a "trigger mechanism" is often used to
minimize such social influences as seduction and
temptation, and to put all the emphasis on something deep and subjective. This is how many experts,
instead of taking a real look, preserve social prefer-

* Even those authors who do consider social and cultural
factors, such as Fromm, Horney, Kardiner, Clara Thompson
or Sullivan, do not go far enough and do not take account
of the full extent of the underlying dynamic interaction between personal and impersonal factors.

ences, profits and prejudices. Whenever *any* particular factor is mentioned, you may run up against vested interests. Of course an emotional conflict may deserve all the emphasis in an individual case. But it may itself just as well be that trigger that activates the inducements to delinquency coming from without.

In other words, it is not realistic to distinguish too schematically between originating and precipitating factors. What is important for understanding current delinquency is that the less social support a youth has, the more he will be at the mercy of untoward impulses. We cannot explain a delinquent act from subjective tendencies alone. There is a fundamental inter-relation of conscious, unconscious and social forces. When we hear so much about the "hostile child" we must realize that, quite apart from his early developmental history, we are dealing with an individual who may receive continuously hostile signals from his social environment. These hostile signals may come via the mass media, via the family, via the school or via the street. Means of influencing children have tremendously increased, yet we still generalize about delinquency according to the same old psychological categories that served twenty-five or thirty years ago. The poet Rainer Maria Rilke said once: "Most people do not know how much splendor there is in the smallest things." One might add that they also do not know how much evil there may be in little things, and how these little things can accumulate to lead to a final effect.

In the study of a social-psychological phenomenon like delinquency, ethical problems cannot be entirely left out. That principle is often overlooked or denied. It is true that it was a great advance when Lombroso went beyond the purely moralistic approach to crime to introduce scientific method. But that does not mean that science is merely a "neutral mechanism" and that ethical questions must be omitted altogether. As J. Bronowski expresses it in his treatise "On Science," such a picture is a caricature and he "who believes it to be true is misled, just as much as the admirer of 'Superman' in the naïve picture stories of the 'comic books.'"

Many considerations connected with delinquency are ethical questions: the right of children to health and education; the minimum standards of physical well-being; protection against seduction in any form; protection against exploitation; the right to fair determination of guilt and punishment. But nowadays it seems that the moral aspects of these questions are apt to be overlooked. There are no ethical problems any more, there are only differences of opinion between psychiatrists! A recent article on delinquency appeared under this headline:

Psychiatrists Differ on Causes
Urge More Research

As I am writing this, I receive a copy of the magazine *Pastoral Psychology* which takes up the comics-and-television question. How does it face this issue? Does it discuss the ethical problems? No. It publishes side by side two reviews of my book *Seduction of the Innocent.* One review, written by Dr. Winfred Overholser, who is superintendent of Saint Elizabeth's Hospital in Washington, D.C., says that there is "incontrovertible evidence" that comic books are a "pernicious influence in the education of the young." The other review says "kids aren't especially influenced to delinquency by what they read" and that if they are they must be "pre-disposed"—a pre-Freudian, ultra-Lombrosian view. The editor of the magazine acknowledges the "concern expressed by many ministers and communities generally" and says that these two reviews "are written by two outstanding psychiatrists, but, as our readers will perceive, they represent two different points of view on the potential affect of comic books on our children." Publishing two divergent opinions by psychiatrists may sound like scientific objectivity; but it is only a refined form of moral evasion.

When with regard to the legal definition of insanity the psychiatrist is asked in court whether the defendant knew the difference between right and wrong, the difficulty is not (as some would have it) that an ethical question is introduced. It is that an ethical question is put so abstractly that it becomes a special task to connect it with clinical facts.

No hard and fast separation exists between delinquency and other childhood troubles. Great confusion is apt to arise when juvenile delinquency is regarded as an entirely distinct and separate entity. One may often read that this or that untoward circumstance may make a child emotionally disturbed, but that it cannot possibly cause juvenile delinquency. How do these authorities know that? On that basis any injurious factor which does not fit into the accepted schemes of what causes juvenile delinquency is arbitrarily excluded. For example, a probation officer testifying before a Senate subcommittee on juvenile delinquency readily accepts "heredity" as a cause of crime, but not what a child "may read or see." It is easy for a child to drift into even serious delinquency. Those experienced in this kind of psychotherapy know that. We don't treat a delinquent, we treat a youth who has committed a delinquent act.

Are delinquents as such mentally abnormal? This is not a problem of sophistry, but a question that has to be frankly faced. There are those who say that all this psychiatric talk is just silly, that delinquents are just cussed mischief-makers who should be taken to the woodshed or the jail. Some even advocate the death penalty for juveniles like Santana. Others assert that delinquents as such are all emotionally ill, that they suffer from neuroses or other definite psychopathological disorders. A supervisor of court casework put it this way to a Senate subcommittee: "Delinquency is a symptom of a sick personality." Still others object to people being "branded normal or abnormal," call this "dualistic thinking" or "all-or-nothing thinking," and say that there is no such thing as normal and abnormal but only "varying shades of gray between the two extremes."

Since I was preparing to testify under oath about such a question, I had to take stock of what the scientific answer is to this question. The best way is to proceed historically. Formerly the sharpest distinction was made between those who are mentally ill and those who are normal. Lombroso, for instance, taught that the criminal (at least what he chose to designate as the "born criminal") was a recognizable, distinctly abnormal type, a product of degeneration or disease, and fundamentally different from normal people. Although this has long been disproved, remnants of this idea keep lingering on in various disguises. It is said, for example, that all criminals are psychopathic personalities, or that all juvenile delinquents suffer from deep emotional disorders or neuroses. Or it is claimed that violence and depravity in the mass media affect only the abnormal child, while the normal, well-adjusted child is assumed to be entirely immune to such influences. These are all obsolete ideas, however fancy the terminology in which they are expressed.

Modern psychiatry and psychoanalysis have shown that the absolute contrast between normal and abnormal cannot be maintained. As far back as 1896 Freud demonstrated that, contrary to prevailing dogma, normal human mechanisms occur in the severest psychosis. Later he spoke of "the supposed gap between the normal and the pathological" which he did so much to fill. In a similar vein the German psychiatrist Kretschmer stated that we "can draw no hard and fast line between normal psychology and psychopathology."

These fundamentally correct ideas have in recent years been so grossly exaggerated that they have led to serious errors, especially in the field of crime and delinquency. To hold that there is no real distinction between normal and abnormal has done specific harm. For example, not one sound clinical study of simulators has been made, and the whole problem is bypassed with the unsubstantiated claim (entirely false in my experience) that all simulators must be pathological. It has also turned out to be very unfair to efface the borders between health and disease for those criminals and delinquents whom we psychiatrists should fight for because definite mental illness has rendered them irresponsible and unaccountable. But the most serious harm done by the crime-is-a-disease school and the delinquency-is-a-deep-emotional-disorder school is the prevalent neglect of the social causes of delinquency. Those who view delinquency in the simple frame of reference of adult neurotics (through a wrong application of otherwise valid psychoanalytic principles) suffer from social myopia.

Under the moral disguise of attention to the individual and the scientific disguise of abnormal psychology we have been neglecting delinquency's social causes. That is understandable, because social and economic forces affect the observer as well as the observed. Both are exposed to social pressures. What we now need is more concreteness and precision in distinguishing between what can be justly called an individual pathological mental condition and social phenomena whose main cause may not lie in individual morbidity.

Special pleading, prejudice, defense of the status quo, vested interests and plain inertia—all these have many disguises. In the scientific study of delinquency

one of the commonest disguises at present is a demand
for an ultra-scientific psuedo-exactness.* Mention
any of the potent factors that help to push youths into
delinquency, such as lack of decent playgrounds,
poverty, indoctrination by mass media or lack of
guidance. You will be told that this is not the "fundamental solution"; not the "basic cause"; not "the pri-
mary cause"; not the "central cause"; not "the whole
cause"; not "the original cause." You will be told that
it is "not directly responsible for delinquency"; that it
is just a precipitating cause for something *much*
deeper; that it is "not a cause for normal healthy children"; that it is not "the cause of delinquency," but
"merely aggravates it." You will be told that it is
"not the cause of delinquency, but both are the result
of something much deeper"; that it is "not the ultimate cause"; that it is not "the basic disorder"; that
it "has no more than an accessory influence and is not
a decisive element"; that delinquency is "so complex
that it is impossible to isolate a single [causal] factor";

* It may for example take the form of the statement in a
recent psychiatric journal that an adequate answer to the
question of whether a TV program is suitable for children
"would require a delicately controlled experiment involving
thousands of cases and extending over a period of years."
That is not how psychiatry was advanced, either by Krae-
pelin or by Freud. It is a misconception of clinical science.
Some TV programs are a potential pathogenic factor, and
we don't need delicacy, nor thousands of cases, nor years,
to determine that. (Cf. *Seduction of the Innocent*. Chapter
XIII.)

that "you cannot pinpoint the exact relationship"; that "there is no direct relationship between delinquency and [*any* factor] *per se.*" This summary, incidentally, is practically a survey of some recent literature on delinquency.

Coupled with all this is the purely theoretical demand that first of all we must answer the question: "Precisely what produces delinquency?"; that we have to look for "cause and effect relationships clearly delineated"; that we must look for "basic," "invariably present" and "specific determinants of delinquency." It is a pity that people get so sidetracked by looking for ultimate causes while missing the problems at hand. With this comes the equally theoretical pronouncement that we must measure the intensity of every causal factor quantitatively and that it shall all be put in statistical form.

Delinquency of the brutal type and extent currently present is an unpleasant aspect of our society. Obviously any causal factor in any way responsible must of necessity be unpleasant to face. So a large part of these scientific-sounding writings, speeches and pronouncements have fundamentally the purpose not of finding causes but of denying them.

Demand for over-precision in the establishment of cause and effect amounts really to the abrogation of valid causality in human relations. This is exactly what characterizes so much that is written about the current outbreak of violence among the youth of this country. We can all save ourselves embarrassment if we say that there are so many factors responsible that not any one of them can be a cause. We are deceiving ourselves by a convenient pluralism. Listen to any speaker on delinquency and you will find that sooner or later he will hide behind the "multiplicity of factors." A typical example occurs in testimony given before a Senate subcommittee: "Myriad factors," the Senators were told, "make up the total personality, and therefore [any factor] only presents one of thousands of influences in the forming of any personality." (The speaker made no attempt to name these "thousands.")

All this amounts to nihilism in the field of prevention and therapy, to the abdication of the scientific method and of the law of causality itself. It is against this that the message of Solferino is directed. We must insist that there are causes in human relations, that they can be disentangled and dealt with. Of course they do not work automatically in iron-clad categories and along a one-line course. A rejecting mother does not have to lead to hostility in the child, nor an alcoholic father to emotional instability in his child. A broken home does not automatically lead to dire consequences for the offspring. On the contrary, it may turn out to be a challenge and an incentive.

The law of causality, in its classical formulation that one cause leads to one effect in the sense that the effect does not occur without the one cause nor the cause without the one effect, exists only in the simplest experiment of physics. The law of causality itself is always valid, but its form and applicability change tremendously. When we proceed from elementary physics to higher physics to natural science to biology and to human relations, we find that everything is connected with everything else. The sequence of causal relations is dynamic and reciprocal. Psychological, economic, political, social, historical, bodily, chemical and other factors work upon one another. That does not mean that we should be diffuse in our thinking. On the contrary, it demands more analysis and more concreteness.

One factor alone *in the absence of all other factors* can never account for a mental abnormality nor a delinquent act. Thus when the former chief of the Children's Bureau in Washington states officially that the saturation of children's minds with crime stories *"per se* in the absence of other factors" will not make a child delinquent, she is saying in effect absolutely nothing at all. It is just a justification for sparing ourselves the trouble of coping with any one preventable abuse now harming children. The Department of Agriculture proceeds more scientifically. They do not have such a bland way of failing to pay attention to pests or threats to the health of fruit trees and livestock.

In recent writings, speeches and reports there is endless repetition of the cliché that "delinquency has multiple causes." Over and over the facile statement is made that "no single factor" should be accused. What that really means is that these writers are afraid to attribute delinquency to *any* factor—and to anything at all; the children are just delinquent. You can always say that there are so many factors that you omit positive and persistent action on any of them. To emphasize above everything else that there are "multiple causes" is just as dogmatic as to single out one factor alone. It is not feasible to determine once and for all "what value to attach to each factor." What may be a powerful and even decisive factor in one case may be relatively insignificant in another. Clinical judgment has to decide in the individual case which of the various factors working upon one another is more significant. From intensive study of significant cases we do know the potential dangers and can guard against them. "The chain of psychopathology," as Dr. Francis Braceland expresses it, "is sometimes no stronger than its weakest link."

It is therefore unscientific to say of any factor which we do not want to acknowledge as a cause that the normal child is so resilient that he cannot be affected by it. An editorial in the New York *Herald Tribune* says: "A normal well-adjusted youngster can probably tolerate a lot of depraved junk without suffering any lasting damage." How do they know that—and is that in any case a decent attitude toward children?

Even in the much simpler field of pharmaceutical substances such a normal type does not exist. The smallest doses of atropine and similar substances can be most helpful with one person yet can cause toxic effects in another. In addition some medicines make certain persons oversensitive to other medicines, again with toxic effects. In the same way the different determining factors in the psychological and social background of a young person may make a child "oversensitive" to all kinds of influences. Surely the balance of a child's mind is as delicate as the balance of his blood pressure. And of that Dr. Irvine Page, president of the American Heart Association, said recently: The mechanisms operating to maintain an even blood pressure are all interrelated. The balance of one cannot be upset without upsetting the balance of the others."

It follows that in determining causal settings we cannot arbitrarily omit any conditions which enter into the picture. For that reason the different disciplines, sociology, psychiatry, psychology, economics, biology, history, cannot be left out of consideration even in the study of the single event that one boy shoots another. Collaboration between them is necessary for the simple reason that the facts with which they deal influence one another mutually.

Psychiatry is not and cannot be the whole answer to delinquency. But at this stage it has important contributions to make. This is true with reference both to interpretation and to the collection of facts. Not everything that is valid can be quantitatively measured and caught in the net of statistics. We no longer proceed only from a patient's symptoms or single acts; we study the whole general evolution of the case. "We must," Dr. David Henderson wrote recently, "pay attention to the background, personal or environmental, in which the symptom is occurring." Not to do so is "a relic of a too concentrated, mechanistic approach." Psychiatry should be dynamic, not dogmatic.

Only a very small number of delinquents needs intensive psychiatric treatment. But all of them need guidance, advice, instruction and encouragement.

The danger is that psychiatrists let themselves be used as an instrument for localizing the blame exclusively within the individual person or within the individual family. The evil that men do comes often from without.

One day when our work was over and I got up from the table in the little room in the jail I asked Santana, "Can I bring you something when I come tomorrow?"

"No," he answered simply and apparently without giving it much attention. But as I was going to the door with him he said suddenly in a low voice, "Bring me some creeps."

IV   *Creeps*

"Never in my life have I come across more disgraceful, more discreditable and more abominable publications than these horror comics."

—Lord Jowitt in the House of Lords debate before passage of the Children and Young Persons (Harmful Publications) Bill in Great Britain

When I saw him the next day, I brought him some chocolate bars. Much as I wanted to please him, I couldn't get myself to bring him the horror comics he had asked me for. He seemed to like the chocolate, and put the bars in his pocket.

I could not get over the impression of discrepancy between this little boy and the big jail with its heavy bars and heavy guards. And there was another incongruity. The prosecution, as the lawyers told me, was working toward an electric-chair sentence and public opinion was actually clamoring for it. Yet Santana did not seem to understand the seriousness of his situation. When I asked him what he wanted to be, he said, in his amiable way, "When I come out of this trouble I want to join the Air Force."

We talked about how he used to put in the time. He went to the movies, for a time he went swimming, he did some boxing. What else did he do for recreation?

"Do you read at all?" I asked him.

"Oh, yes," he replied. "I read a lot. In Puerto Rico I read Spanish and English, and here too. But more in English here."

"What do you read?"

"Funny books. Creeps."

"What other books did you read?"

"I don't read other books."

"Never?"

"No, I only read the creeps."

"Tell me about that."

"I read them in Puerto Rico, too. But not so many. In Puerto Rico I did not pay so much attention to them.

In New York I read a lot. I used to have a closet full. Some guys gave them to me, some I bought."

"What was the largest number you had at one time?"

"Two hundred or three hundred."

This may sound incredible to those who have not studied the children-comic book problem. But I have seen many children like that. And only recently in Indiana when a group of public-spirited people offered every child a real book for ten comic books, one boy appeared with 490! So they had to make the rule that one hundred comic books was the maximum allowed each child.

Santana told me that he read about five creeps every day. Some of them he read "many times." I asked him to tell me all the titles that he could remember. This seemed hard for him to do. After some thought he gave me, slowly, this list:

> The Vault Creep
> The Vault of Fear
> Crime Book
> Crime Does Not Pay
> Superman
> Bat Man
> Cowboys
> Mysteries

I asked him to tell me some of the actual stories. He wrinkled his forehead even more. "Five guys, they went robbing."

"What did they do?"

"In each book are five or six murders. I don't like it if somebody gets killed."

"Why do you read them?"

"They are the only comic books that are something good to read. They are the kind that are around. I don't like the love comics."

"Why not read other books?"

"I can't read books with no pictures. I have no interest in those. You feel bored, like."

"Which comic books do you like best?"

"The creeps are my favorites."

"What's so interesting about the creeps?"

"They always do something wrong and drive the people crazy. Where somebody kills another person. So the creep make the person who die rise up again and kill the guy who killed."

"What else?"

"That's all. There is always something about the creeps and always killing them."

"What do the police do?"

"In the creeps there is no police."

"Who calls them *creeps?*"

"That's the name of the funny books."

"What do the girls do in them?"

"Sometimes the guy kills the girl and she rises up again and kill him. The man kills the girl and then she kills him."

"How is that possible?"

"She comes back from the grave."

"What else?"

"A man drinks a girl's blood—no, a girl drinks a man's blood—I don't remember. In all the funny books

I told you, there is only killing in them. Sometime the people when they know somebody killed, they go after him to beat him up with sticks, pipes, rifles, bottles, every kind of weapons."

"What else?"

"People sees somebody killing another person. They come and beat him up. In the comic books they go against the Mexicans. The American people make war against the Mexicans. They kill each other."

"Anything else?"

"Someone they cut the head off." (He pointed to his neck.) "Sometimes the head talks back to the guy who cut it."

"What does it say?"

"I don't remember what he says. They steal and rob and kill."

These are the boy's words just as I took them down. It may not be legal evidence; but it certainly is clinical evidence. Suppose a patient on the psychoanalytic couch were to tell us these stories as his fantasies. Would we not regard them as definitely morbid and do everything to get him into a condition where he could get rid of them? To adults we offer a cure; to children we sell the disease.

It seemed to me that I had come across another incongruity, another paradox. Here was a young boy, quiet, unobtrusive, anxious to please and to conform. So what do we do? We fill his mind to the brim with stories that are what John Crosby has so well characterized as plain ordinary commercialized sadism. I convinced myself that Santana was steeped in this lore.

The Senate Juvenile Delinquency Subcommittee recently reported that the impact of comic books is not so serious as that of movies and television because they "must be sought out" and "demand strong imaginary projections" (whatever that may mean). But in town and country children cannot escape seeing these comics. Their distribution (often coercive) is ubiquitous. Children come across them in the general store, the candy store, at the dentist's, in school, at church parties, in clinics and hospitals, in their friends' homes, at newsstands, at the ice-cream parlor. How can a child escape seeing them and being tempted by them? Especially in segregated neighborhoods, where many Puerto Ricans live, comic books are practically foisted upon them. I have seen it myself and I know many of these creeps.

Here are some samples: A man starves his wife to death and marries a young girl who then starves him to death.

A woman dug out of her grave gives birth to a baby.

A ghoul who murders girls at night turns out to be the detective in charge of the case.

A guest appears on a television panel show with two young men and a woman. They kill him and drink his blood.

A girl kills her lover, claiming she mistook him for an escaped criminal. Later the criminal comes and kills her.

A boy takes eight different girls successively for a ride in his car and kills them. He escapes punishment because he is a supernatural being.

A nephew and niece kill their aunt for money. The aunt returns from the grave and kills them both.

What is important about all this is the quantity and the endless repetition of these violent images. The *British Medical Journal* has described these (American) creeps like this: "Just occasionally the merely weird is left to stand in dim contrast to the homicidal clatter that fills the pages; but the ordinary run of stories almost without exception in some of the comics, are concerned with violent, painful, brutal death." I computed that since Santana had been in the United States, in the comic books that he had read and in the movies that he had attended, he had seen at least 22,000 homicides. That is what we pumped into this boy's head. I am not counting assaults, threats, rapes, tortures and other assorted violence. I also leave out what he saw on television— though that would have supplemented his education in violence—because the family had not had their television set very long. At first glance there seems to be a discrepancy between what we teach him and what we want to do to him when he does what we have taught him. Actually, though, there is no discrepancy: we teach him to kill and then when he does it, we try to kill him—just like a plot in the creeps.

I had to ask myself this question: Could I testify before the jury about this boy's mind without mentioning what had been put into it? It seemed to me that that would be both unscientific and untruthful.

It is unfortunate for American children—and it seemed to me that at least to some extent Santana was one of the victims of this circumstance—that the official guardians of mental health are so reluctant to acknowledge the damage done by the glorification of brutality and violence in mass media (of which the comics are merely the most glaring example). The effect of mass media has created an entirely new clinical situation. I had just received a big volume called *Evaluation of Mental Health* from the United States Department of Health, Education and Welfare, National Institute of Mental Health (1955). In it are summarized 984 papers and articles, mentioning all sorts of factors affecting mental health. There is *no mention whatsoever* of the evaluation of mass media as a mental health factor. Is it scientific, is it fair, to ignore completely these mass pressures on children?

Clinical evidence is not what we put through the wringer of statistics, but is what a person says. One reason why mass media are not referred to in this official report is not far to seek. The book contains a number of basic assumptions. One goes as follows: "An understanding of causality in human behavior is more effective in improving mental health than its emphasis on surface effects." It is arbitrary in the extreme to distinguish so sharply between what is here called "causality" and "surface effects." Goethe combatted this rigid metaphysical dualism long ago:

> Nature has neither kernel nor shell,
> She's both in one, the truth to tell.

Causality in human relations operates in intricate ways. What may *appear* to be merely a "surface effect" may be an important contributing *causal* factor.

Any "basic assumption" that pompously rules out a whole set of observations is unscientific. Such an approach is far removed from the actual life of the people. Boys like Santana find no place in it.

To say the least, the psychological diet provided by the mass media was not good for Santana. At what precise moment a wrong diet begins to do harm cannot be determined either in the physical or mental sphere. But once it does do harm it affects the whole person. It is strange, therefore, to read this conclusion in a 1954 senate subcommittee report: "Through television, radio, movies, and comics, children are fed a heavy diet of violence and crime. . . . Whether or not such programs also influence a child's attitude toward the standards of society is a matter to be explored." How could a "heavy diet of violence and crime" fail to have such an influence? Perhaps instead of the attitude of the child, what should be explored are the standards of society.

Santana's reading of creeps was the normal learning of abnormal subject matter. His impressionable and flexible mind was conditioned by situations he would not have met in an entire lifetime. It is clear that his reading of creeps became an unhealthy addiction. It would be quite wrong to look for the causes of this addiction exclusively in the boy.

Crime creeps and comics are habit-forming and are designed to be habit-forming. They heap excitement upon excitement, without any "filler" (the mass media term for artistic details). Many intelligent children whom I have asked have told me they read them because they couldn't break away from them.

Reading creeps was part of Santana's Americaniza-
tion. At least so it appeared to him. He was learning.
At any rate, he was trying to learn. One lesson we
instilled in him by way of comics and movies is that
violence is not a problem but a solution. It is a method
to be used. As Geoffrey Handley-Taylor put it (the
message is that) "only through lawlessness and violence can one get things done." In Santana's mind the
comics' message was reinforced by the movies and
vice versa, and both by the lessons from the street.
Seeds of violence were planted in his mind, where they
might otherwise never have appeared.

Since he had told me that he had read only comics,
and not any books, I gave him some reading tests
(Gray's Oral Reading and Monroe Silent Reading
Test). He was fully familiar with English and could
read short bits well enough. But he failed when asked
to read one whole page in a book. When I asked him
to write, he also did well enough, but made spelling
mistakes typical of children who read comic books
exclusively. For years I have been getting letters from
children approving or disapproving my criticism of
comic books. Invariably the chronic comics readers
are the bad spellers. Inability to read a page of text
comes from the same source, as I described in the
chapter on "Reading" in *Seduction of the Innocent*.
Comic books promote picture-gazing instead of reading, and what text there is occurs in broken lines, in
bubbles or in balloons with handles. Comic books are
the Esperanto of the illiterate.

As my picture of Santana's character became
clearer in my conversations with him, it was incongru-

ous to hear him talk about these stories from the creeps. We do to these children exactly the opposite of what Maxim Gorky advised in his writings on children's literature: "We should create in children contempt and aversion for crime, not excitement and anxiety about it." Santana's whole social balance was a delicate one. He was confused about what standards he should cling to. The creeps did not help him to clarify his ethical perspective. It is often said that we do not know enough about the effect of mass media. Do we really know so little about it? Surely the long history of philosophy, religion, education, political propaganda and advertising have taught us a lot of both the good and the bad influences of pictures and the written word. Santana did not have enough mental resources to withstand the influences which so fascinated him. This ethical confusion made it infinitely harder for him to remain non-delinquent and—although it is so fashionable to blame mothers— it made it harder for his mother to keep him out of trouble.

What, I asked myself, was the effect of his comics reading on the crime? I felt that it was one piece in a larger mosaic.

V   *Terror*

"The only individuals we know are individuals-in-society."

—Tolstoi

Frank had given me the telephone number of his aunt, his mother's sister. "My mother can only speak Spanish," he said. "But my aunt can speak Spanish and English." I arranged with this aunt a meeting at Mrs. Santana's apartment so that she could interpret for us.

Early one evening Santana's lawyer and I arrived at the crowded street where the Santanas lived. We walked up some steep wooden steps to the front entrance of the house and rang the bell of the apartment. At once the door opened a little and a booming male voice shouted, "*You* are the Killer! And he is the witness to prove it!" We were both more than a little startled. Mrs. Santana opened the door wider and greeted us politely. Right there was a television screen and in front of it sprawled on chairs in rapt fascination were the two boys, Santana's brothers.

The television melodrama continued loudly and I suggested to tall fifteen-year-old José that it be turned a little lower. Later at somebody's suggestion it was turned off entirely. The apartment was neat and tidy. There were two rooms which could be separated by a curtain. One was the bedroom where Mrs. Santana slept, the other the living room where evidently the boys slept. There was no kitchen and no bathroom. I was seated on a couch which they told me was Frank's bed at night. The rooms were simply furnished, but everything was kept spick and span. In the bedroom were several religious pictures, and on a commode in a corner a votive candle was burning. In the living room there were also pictures on the wall, one an engraving of a storm-twisted California pine.

I had seen that before. It struck me as beautiful and somewhat appropriate for this storm-twisted family.

Frank's mother was only thirty-eight, but looked much older. She was thin, frail and tired. She had worked in a dressmaking factory at wages with which she could just make both ends meet. She told me she had earned between fourteen and sixteen dollars a week. She had had to change her apartment several times since coming to New York and that was always a difficult chore, even with their few belongings. Since November, 1951, she had been sick. She couldn't tell me exactly what was wrong with her. She said the doctor had told her that she was too thin and that she couldn't work. She felt dizzy and tired, and her stomach bothered her and she vomited sometimes. I asked what medical care she got. She told me she was attending a hospital clinic. The last time she had been there was in April, 1954. She showed me her clinic card on which there was an appointment for September (!) which she evidently had not kept.

Mrs. Santana confirmed practically all that her son had told me. She had to coax him to eat. He was not happy like the other children. That had been so even in Puerto Rico. He was always quiet (*siempre callado*). Sometimes he appeared *triste*. She also confirmed that he started things and then gave them up —first the swimming, then the exercises with the weights she had bought him, then the boxing. "He was good with his hands—fixed his bicycle and those of other boys." At this point José brought in the lamp Frank had made. Several times during the conversation the aunt, the interpreter, broke in to say, "I know that, too."

I have often had to talk with mothers of delinquents and I am always impressed with what a rotten deal they get. It is so easy to blame them on the basis of all the theoretical clichés about mother-child relationships. But how rarely does anyone listen to them, and how rarely does anyone help them! I got the impression that she was not trying to use the occasion to give me any embellished picture of Frank. She wanted to tell me how he really was. She conveyed to me a picture of Frank as a passive boy, not given to anger, always kind and courteous and nice to people, never in fights. Until recent months he had obeyed her. She had had no idea that he was not going to school until a truant officer had told her so a few months before. Frank's father had died December 12, 1941. She showed me the death certificate. He had died after an operation for an intestinal obstruction.

I remembered Frank's creeps and told José that Frank had told me about them. They were still there where he had left them, and José brought them to me. There were twenty-three comic books in the bunch he gave me. Nine were in Spanish, fourteen were in English. Of the latter, all but three had the much-advertised Seal of Approval of the comic-book industry, "Approved by the Comics Code Authority." There was little difference between those with and those without the Seal. For example, one with the Seal had no less than thirty-two (32) pictures in which a gun is used! The impression any child would get from this comic book is that only a man with a gun *is* a man.

There are also such choice bits in balloons as this:

Ten hours before Fred Wharton had strangled a man, but that man was old, feeble.

There were advertisements teaching violence:

> YOU, TOO, CAN BE TOUGH!
> . . . all the secrets, grips, blows,
> pressures, jabs, tactics, etc. . . .
> HITTING WHERE IT HURTS . . .
>
> _____
>
> Elbow Jab, Knee Jab . . .

Other advertisements offer weapons:

> guns, supplies
> knives
> throwing knives

Premium ads addressed to "BOYS" offer "genuine 22 caliber rifles." There were the advertisements that make children self-conscious about their build (which so preoccupied Santana anyway):

> COME ON, BUDDY, QUIT BEING A
> BAG-OF-BONES WEAKLING . . .
>
> _____

I improved my HE-MAN looks 1,000% . . .
I gained 70 lbs. of mighty muscle*

or

TIRED OF BEING ASHAMED OF YOUR BUILD?
. . . how ashamed are you of your present
physical condition?

Comic books in Spanish are particularly harmful. They are offered to Puerto Rican children in New York in profusion. Often they are not taught well how to read English, and "reading" Spanish comics hinders their learning even more. As one boy said, "I don't have to know the word for 'bosom' or for 'gun,' I don't need it. I can see it from the pictures."

One of Santana's comic books in Spanish had a half-page illustration of a nude light-skinned man stretched on a primitive stone altar, held down by dark-skinned figures who seem to be cutting his heart out. This is presented as a lesson in history. These Spanish comic books are sold to the doubly defenseless Puerto Rican children who live in segregated areas for fifteen cents, instead of the usual ten-cent comic-book price.

As we looked over these comic books the lawyer took out his fountain pen and wrote on each of them

---

* This is medically impossible, hence a fraudulent claim. If the post office protected children's health as assiduously as adults' morals, this could not be sent through the mails.

his name, the date and the time of day. (It was seven thirty P.M.) That would prove that they *were* Santana's, and I intended to offer them all in evidence so the jury could judge for themselves what influence they had on the boy's mind.

I tried to picture how it was when Frank was home. Despite his father's death this could have been a happy family. Certainly the conscientious mother tried hard to do everything she could. But what help did this family get? It has been determined that in an area like this one in the Bronx about half of the families receiving welfare assistance are on the rolls because one adult member of the family is ill. Mrs. Santana certainly did not receive the medical assistance she should have. She was in need of treatment. Maybe she needed a special diet. No social worker had ever checked up on why she didn't go to the hospital clinic any more, although her last visit was over a year ago. Knowing these clinics, how patients have to wait and how many patients one doctor sometimes has to go over, it is easy to understand why a patient drops out. Medically Mrs. Santana was just a statistic, and as far as curability and rehabilitation were concerned, probably a wrong one.

I ascertained later, through the social-service exchange, that not one social agency had had any contact with this family! There was nobody who listened to what worried the mother or what was on the mind of the boy. Only after the shot had been fired did any agency pay any attention to them. What happened was not the neglect of a routine, but the routine of neglect. I know from many years of experience in clinics that what we are given to understand these public and private social agencies do for people is painted in colors far rosier than reality. There is an enormous amount of evasion and, as it is called, buck-passing.

There are many reasons why an agency does not take a case: wrong religion; wrong color (on forms, the words *Puerto Rican* are filled in under the heading: "Color"); case too serious; case not serious enough; patient's I.Q. too low; mother not co-operative (mother "not workable"); wrong area of the city; "does not fit into our research program." All these excuses I have heard literally hundreds of times. The agencies make long charts and records, and write reports to one another. Here is a typical letter from a psychiatrist in a mental hygiene clinic to a social agency referring to a case in the Bronx: "It was our conclusion that inasmuch as this boy's maladjustment and behavior difficulties stemmed from the cultural and situational factors in the home it was doubtful if he would benefit from treatment in our clinic." Case rejected.

Or a leading social agency, in an official letter, expresses its "discouragement in the face of intellectual limitations of the mother and the poor social environment," and states "While we recognize that the opportunities offered these children for development are poor environmentally, we also see that the limitations are too great to indicate any progress through case work." Case closed.

There is also a stupendous amount of duplication which usually leads not to the work being done twice, but to its not being done at all. Many of the statistics

of clinics and social agencies are misleading. Philan-
thropy tempered by chaos.

All this is hidden under an overlay of fancy terminology in reports and projects. For example, we read
about "interpreting the agency to the family" and, on
a higher governmental level, about "building a
bridge to the community." Hours of committee meetings and many printed pages are devoted to such
doubletalk. If you want to help people really, you
don't have much interpreting to do. The reason why
families don't return to agencies is that they feel that
what they get is not understanding but reproaches
and peering into their lives. Children with wrong
"cultural and situational factors in the home" (which
frequently is a euphemism for race prejudice affecting Negroes, Puerto Ricans and other minorities) are
often not sent for psychotherapy at all.

Frank certainly gave enough warning that some
help and guidance was necessary. He was not satis-
fied with the vocational work assigned to him. He
needed and deserved either an explanation or a better assignment. He is not an isolated case. The vocational guidance and training programs are apt to be
unrealistic. The equipment in vocational high schools
is often obsolete and poor. If the pupils later get jobs,
they have to be trained again from the beginning. Too
many are trained for a type of work where there is
little chance of later employment. Gifted Negro and
Puerto Rican children are often steered away from
academic high schools and advised by teachers or
guidance counsellors to take some manual industrial
course because they wouldn't get a better job any-

how. Not only the fact but the way it is done is often
traumatic.

How much truancy must a boy practice before he
comes to the attention of the Bureau of Attendance?
And even then who bothers to ascertain sympathet-
ically why a boy plays truant? How must he behave
to get some—even the most cursory—mental-hygiene
attention? Frank did fairly well in English. Had it
been made easy for him to learn English? Puerto Rican
children who are in an exclusively Spanish-speaking
class are handicapped because they do not learn
English from other children. And the avalanche of
comics in Spanish does not help, either. Except for
the barely enough money from the Department of
Welfare, the community brought nothing to this family except murder *via* television and comic books.

As we were about to leave, there was some kind of
commotion. Mrs. Santana and the aunt talked to
each other eagerly and then first the one, then
the other, left the room and came back. The interpreter explained to me that Mrs. Santana was anxious for me to meet an acquaintance of theirs. Would
I be willing to speak to him? Of course I would.

Soon the man came in. He was below middle age,
a blond, heavy-set, typical, average U.S. citizen. We
sat down together. He said he had come in at Mrs.
Santana's request to speak to me. He was friendly,
open-faced, sincere. "Of all the boys around here,"
he said, "Frank was the best-mannered. You didn't
have to ask him to do anything. He always helped
you if you needed him.

"There were very good points in him. Anything I

told him he listened to. I wish I had known that he was playing hooky or had any trouble. I could have talked to him and he would have listened to me."

From the way he spoke it was apparent that he meant what he said, that he liked the boy. "Of all the boys around here, he was the best. Only, you know, the woman was handicapped. Today you need a man's hand. You know his mother is sick. I know her. She is doing the best she can. If only I had known! The mothers don't get the cards from school. If I had known he was playing hooky I would have told him!"

I thanked him for dropping in. He could see that I was interested and taking me a little aside became more confidential: "You know what it really is," he said, gesticulating with his right arm. "It's the trouble they make with Puerto Ricans. It's a complex affair on this block. There are colored, Spanish and white here. Frank needed guidance. The Navajos were founded in this block. We've had gangs here for several years. Make no mistake about it, this is an area where they *have* to have a gang. On this block there is a complete division between Puerto Ricans and others. The Puerto Ricans can't go here or there because there are other boys. If a Puerto Rican boy walks in a white area—! Then the trouble really starts! You have to analyze all groups, and the woman was not in a position to analyze all the groups. This is a lingering thing. The fires can die but the embers are still there. It isn't these kids, it's the grownups. If it weren't for the feeling of the whites against the Puerto Ricans, that gang trouble wouldn't exist at all in this area! Frank is a good kid. Make no mistake about that."

I thanked him again for all the information. Then I explained to him how valuable it would be to refer to his opinion of Frank when I testified in court. "I can refer to it," I said. "But I cannot quote you because that would be against the rules of the court, the rules of evidence. The lawyers would call it 'hearsay.' So I want to ask you: please come into court and just say what you know about Frank's character. That would be a great help in his case."

The man's whole attitude changed at once, suddenly. There was extreme dread in his face. "Oh, no!" he said with great emphasis.

"Maybe you don't understand exactly what I mean," I said. I couldn't help noticing his alarm.

"Oh, yes, I do," he answered.

"I can see you are a decent person," I said. "You have no prejudice. Maybe you don't realize that this boy's life might depend on your testimony. All I would like you to say is what you told me—that Frank is a good kid."

He shook his head decidedly. "No. I couldn't possibly go into a court. And you can't mention my name, either. You don't know how people feel against these Puerto Ricans."

"But you are different," I said. "Why don't you say a good word for him when it might mean so much?"

By now this good-natured man looked really upset. "I'll tell you why," he retorted. "If I say a good word about this boy, I'd lose my job! Don't you see? I have a family to think of!"

So this was the social climate in which Santana lived. I felt that I had gotten an important clue to the dynamics of his case.

We were ready to go. Carrying Frank's comic books under my arm, I looked once more around the two rooms. There was the couch that served as his bed, the California pine on the wall, the flickering votive candle in the corner. We all shook hands and said good-bye.

We walked down the wooden steps from the front door. On the street the lawyer turned to me: "Would you think a man like that would be so scared? Now what do you call *that?*"

"That," I said, "is terror."

VI   *The Discovery of Puerto Rico*

"Against nature no man can assert a right, but in the state of society neediness immediately takes on the form of an injustice."

—Hegel

On November 15, 1493, Columbus discovered Puerto Rico. Many Americans do not seem to have discovered it yet.

The island was originally called Boriquén. Columbus named it Isla de San Juan Bautista, the Isle of St. John the Baptist. Later from its main harbor, now San Juan, the whole island was called Puerto Rico, the rich port. As a result of oppression by Spain, there were revolts and the largest part of the population—according to some historians six hundred thousand—was wiped out. In the second half of the eighteenth century the Island began to recover and in the early nineteenth century it started to flourish. Toward the end of the nineteenth century it became more and more independent from Spain and it had reached a degree of autonomy* when, after the Spanish-American War, it was annexed by the United States. When General Miles landed at the head of the invading

---

* As a Puerto Rican historian, Tomás Blanco, puts it (1955): "At the very moment when the Puerto Rican people were about to undergo a new stage of mature development in harmony with their past, they suffered the violence of a shocking change, through a war with the declaration of which they had nothing to do, through the rigor of a defeat in which they had no part, and through the provisions of a peace treaty in negotiations for which they had neither voice nor vote. In the face of overwhelming arms and the ruthless demands of the victor, they were subjugated as a people from having been an autonomous province, and they became, as the spoils of war, the colony of a foreign and powerful nation."

American forces in 1898 he said in a proclamation: "We have come to bring you protection, not only to yourselves but to your property (and) to promote your prosperity."

How did that work out for the people of Puerto Rico? According to the authoritative study *Puerto Rico's Economic Future* by Harvey S. Perloff (University of Chicago Press. 1950) "the condition of the masses of the Island people in the period 1899-1927 could be described as deplorable" and "the situation of the Puerto Rican people between 1928 and 1940 can only be described as bordering on the critical." Note that this includes the prosperity era after the First World War. Until the regime of Franklin D. Roosevelt the Island was officially called Porto Rico; only then did it become entitled to the correct spelling of its name. What happened during the Depression of the thirties, when Santana was born, can be envisaged from the single fact that pay "amounted to 3 cents per dozen (!) for hand embroidering and hemming handkerchiefs" (Hanson. 1955). In later promotional brochures which do not include this sort of detail, such activities are described like this: "More than 70,000 nimble-fingered men and women produce handkerchiefs . . . and other items."

Describing conditions inside Puerto Rico in 1941, when Santana was four years old, John Gunther calls it "our orphan island" and says: "Its poverty is a disgrace to the Stars and Stripes. . . . What I found appalled me. [Scenes that are] a shame and disgrace to the United States. . . . To see it [misery, disease, squalor, filth] on American territory, among people whom the United States has governed since 1898, in a region for which our federal responsibility has been complete for 43 years, is a paralyzing jolt to anyone who believes in American standards of progress and civilization." He goes on to say that infant mortality in Puerto Rico is the highest in the world and that the average income of the peasant is about $135.00 a year, or less than 40 cents a day. Good reporter that he is, he gives this graphic detail: "The daily per capita consumption of milk in the United States is three-quarters of a pint. In Puerto Rico it is exactly one teaspoonful." Puerto Rican children (as Robert Morss Lovett expressed it) were also intellectually undernourished. One reason for this was that by bureaucratic orders from Washington the educational authorities of Puerto Rico had to arrange for instruction in high school to be in English in all subjects. Lovett, who studied this situation, came to the conclusion that "this unfortunate experiment" had "evil effects on education in general."

In 1917 Puerto Ricans were granted formal American citizenship and thirty years later the right to elect their own governor. Two years later, in 1949, their first governor was elected by the people, Luis Muñoz Marín, who is governor now.

In 1952 Puerto Rico got a constitution. It is noteworthy that the United States Congress did not permit the Puerto Rican constitution to stand as drafted, but removed certain provisions (Hanson. 1955): *e.g.,* "the right of every pregnant or nursing mother and child to care and special aid." At the same time it attained the status of a Commonwealth. This was called Estado Libre Asociado (Associated Free State). This political status is unique in the history of relationships between countries. It is an "experiment in non-independent independence" (Hanson. 1955). There are some who believe that the constitution and Commonwealth status present a long-range final solution. Others recognize it as a makeshift with considerable economic injustice for the Puerto Ricans. They point out that Puerto Rico would be better off if it had the right to produce and export without restrictions, trade freely with whom, wherever and however it wanted, to buy on the cheapest market and use shipping at the most advantageous rates. As it is, in 1955 Puerto Rico is forced to be the world's largest per capita consumer of United States products.

In recent years Puerto Rico has unquestionably made considerable strides forward in various fields. But the set-up of the Associated Free State makes it much more "associated" than "free." In local courts in Puerto Rico the official language is Spanish. According to Federal law (made by the United States Congress where there are no Puerto Rican representatives), in trials for a Federal offense English is the official language and only a person with full knowledge of the English language can be on the jury list. A majority of Puerto Ricans cannot fulfill this requirement so they cannot be on such juries, although they are tried by them. And a person may be tried without understanding a word of the proceedings.

For very many people in Puerto Rico economic conditions are still deplorable. This is not so much a hangover as fundamentally a continuation of previous conditions. In 1942 outside of the largest cities one physician had to care for more than ten thousand patients. According to the Department of Health of Puerto Rico in 1952, 57 per cent of the people who died had no medical attention at all. In 1943 nearly one half of the population was unemployed (Goshal. 1948)—this when, according to Tomás Blanco, absentee North American corporations have paid "fabulous dividends of 115%."

Fortune magazine a few years ago had an enlightening article on the industrialization of Puerto Rico. It was appropriately called "Profit Hunters in Puerto Rico." This profit hunt has now been going on in one form or another for over half a century. I know of a large textile plant which in the first two years of its operation was able to write off the entire original cost of the firm's establishment on the Island. This was made possible primarily by the very low wages paid native labor.

In the continental United States Puerto Rican laborers have been grossly taken advantage of, as some recent investigations (far from complete) have made clear. I know instances where in town and country Puerto Ricans have to work much longer hours and get less pay than others in the same jobs. They get lower wages, for instance, in "store front factories" (the modern sweatshops) where subcontractors manufacture garments.

In recent sociological literature a new term has appeared: "Puertoricanization." It refers to a peculiar state of economic, legal, administrative and military relationships with a larger nation which is neither colonial nor non-colonial. Whereas Puerto Rico is in name not a colony, it is not unlike one in operation. That there is some dissatisfaction with this has been demonstrated by some desperate terroristic acts in Washington. It has been said in this connection that "every once in a while real bullets come out of the unreal world and kill real people." But as far as I can see, except for individual cases of insanity, bullets always come from an all-too-real world.

It is almost impossible to speak to anybody about Puerto Ricans or to read any recent literature about them without being confronted with the question: Why do they come here? It is a most unfair question. Puerto Ricans come to the United States for the same reason that all other people have been coming here for many years. They want to create a better life for themselves and for their children. The only difference is that Puerto Ricans are not even immigrants in the strict sense, since they are already American citizens when they come here. In all modern countries there has been a tendency for members of the rural population to migrate to small towns and then to large towns. If conditions were overwhelmingly difficult there was a trend to migrate to countries of greater opportunity. On the day before Santana's trial was to begin, it was reported in *The New York Times* that almost one half of the Island's total labor force was either under-employed or totally unemployed. For instance, a needle worker earning fifty-five cents an hour may get only two or three days' work in a week.

Many Puerto Ricans have made an excellent adjustment in the United States and in New York. They work hard and have good incomes. They are integrated in their communities and they have added to the stream of American culture some of their own partly Spanish-derived heritage. This large number is completely overlooked when we hear so much about the "Puerto Rican problem." Through my work in clinics I had been familiar for many years with the prejudice against Puerto Ricans. It is a real pre-judice, a pre-judgment of individuals on the basis of preconceived notions.

Prejudice against Puerto Ricans is most outspoken in New York City, where many Puerto Ricans live; but it is more or less the same in other parts of the country. When I spoke to people about the Santana case, and read about Puerto Ricans, all these prejudices showed up. There was in the general population a hysterical fear of them. Even liberal people who prided themselves on their broadmindedness were nervous and impatient when this subject came up.

It is a well-established axiom of psychology that where there is an excess of emotion there must be powerful dynamic motives at work. The attitude against Puerto Ricans is not based on fact and rational observation, but on national and race prejudice. Experienced social scientists pointed out long ago that if we penetrate to the deepest roots of these attitudes, there are in the last analysis economic motives which divide people and set them against one another.

That national and race prejudice is the prime factor in the so-called Puerto Rican problem is vigorously denied and obscured by high-sounding phrases. Even the word *prejudice* is disguised by apologetic social scientists by the elegant five-dollar word "ethnocentrism." And there is an endless succession of fancy expressions such as "subcultures," "ethnic tensions," "acculturation programs," "transculturative processes," "cross-cultural surveys," "different cultural streams," "intercultural relations," and so on. All this phraseology serves the purpose of obscuring very simple facts. For prejudice is now explained and justified by being clad in the scientific garb of psychopathology and sociology.

The main complaint against Puerto Ricans is that there are too many of them, both on the Island and in the United States! This complaint is made with particular vehemence and with absolute conviction, not only by the man in the street and the newspapers, but even in scientific literature. It is emphasized with astonishing unanimity and monotony in every recent American utterance about Puerto Ricans. In a 1953 study published by the American Academy of Political and Social Science and entitled "Puerto Rico, A Study in Democratic Development" the whole material is grouped under only four sections—and one of the four is "TOO MANY PEOPLE." In 1955 in the New York *Times Magazine* an article "Puerto Rico, Land of Paradox," the too-many-Puerto-Ricans theme occurs no less than five times: "too many people"; "to cope with the population's growth"; "the population problem"; "the birth-rate"; "a decline in the birth-rate is necessary." In other writings this theme occurs over and over: "the increasing density of population"; "to check the rate of population increase in the cultural setting of Puerto

Rico"; "the population problem"; "over-population." One preferred word almost obscene in its condescending social use is "fertility": "the higher fertility of Puerto Ricans"; "uncontrolled fertility"; "runaway fertility"; "primitive fertility."

One characteristic detail is that death rate and birth rate of Puerto Ricans are discussed together as if both were evils. For instance, the statement was made at the National Conference of Social Work (a few days before I examined Santana in jail) that "though the birth rate has decreased from 39 in 1940 to 34.8 in 1953, it has not done so to the extent that death rates have" (sic!). We read about successful efforts to reduce the death rate in Puerto Rico coupled with unabashed statements that progress demands that we do exactly the same thing with the birth rate. It has even been suggested as a solution for the population problem that television facilities should be expanded in Puerto Rico so that the people there would stay up later and spend less time in bed!

It seems that Puerto Ricans are not evaluated, but counted. Much of the discussion about Puerto Ricans boils down to propaganda against propagation. Their numbers are used not only as a reproach but as a "scientific" explanation of all problems connected with them. Their numbers explain their living conditions both in Puerto Rico and on the continent; their numbers explain all their troubles. Of course that is also the explanation for their "fantastic rate of immigration."

It is one thing to advise birth control to an individual family or to make such information generally available. But it is totally different to advise it as a panacea for the social and economic problems of a hard-pressed people. Surgeons report that sterilization operations (cutting the tubes) is now one of the most frequent operations in Puerto Rico. In the American mission hospital (Ryder Memorial Hospital) it is performed many times a week for birth-control purposes, with the only restriction that it is not done on women with fewer than three children.

One cannot solve social problems with biological methods. However disguised the too-many-Puerto-Ricans argument may be, there is consciously or unconsciously a race-derogatory element behind it. However modern the language and however documented the assertions, one can recognize in all these diagnoses, remedies and proposals what Harold Cox, editor of the *Edinburgh Review,* years ago said more frankly: "If the lower races continue to multiply, while the higher races restrict their numbers, the time will come when the mastery of the world will pass to the inferior but more prolific types of mankind."

By the spoken and printed word, Puerto Ricans are accused of many things. "We are afraid of them," an educated woman said to me, a woman who is the mother of two college-age children. "They are so many, and they are so dangerous." The defense, to the limited extent that it exists at all, is half-hearted and half-apologetic. One fashionable accusation is that Puerto Ricans are responsible for a large part of juvenile delinquency, and especially for its current violence. This is widely believed; but there is no evidence for it whatsoever. One reason for this belief is that all the negative things about Puerto Ricans are publicized, while no mention is made of how hard they work, how hard they try to adjust and how devoted they are to their children—who also try hard to adjust, just as other children do. Puerto Rican youths commit proportionately fewer serious delinquencies. In Puerto Rico warring juvenile gangs do not exist and the devotion of adults to children is exemplary. Abandonment of infants or children is totally unknown there. This includes children born out of wedlock. The incidence of juvenile delinquency in Puerto Rico is extraordinarily small. According to figures given out by the Department of Health there, in 1954, the percentage of "arrests [for juvenile delinquency] for the whole Island for a population of children around 1,000,000" is .0017.

There is a host of other accusations. It is said, for example, that the Puerto Rican, "a product of cultural and racial conflict on his Island, produces further ethnic conflict in New York." This may sound persuasive but it puts matters upside down. There is in effect practically no racial conflict on the Island, and in New York the Puerto Rican does not produce the conflict, but is the victim of it. In the very neighborhood where Santana lived there have been "near race-riots against Puerto Ricans." They are accused of working for less money and thereby taking jobs from other people. They are accused of coming to the United States in order to get on relief. They are supposed to seek out the most dilapidated housing deliberately and cause its further deterioration.

Among the more detailed accusations are that they live too crowded in apartments, that they are unsanitary, that they are careless about garbage disposal, that trees in nice nieghborhoods are cut down on account of them, that they dress differently from others, that they have earlier sex experiences than others. All these accusations are either entirely baseless or distorted, especially with regard to cause and effect. To say that Puerto Ricans come to this country in order to get on relief is slander. That they receive more relief than other people is a myth. Official figures show (March 1955) that 92 per cent of the Puerto Rican population is self-supporting. Considering the poor circumstances many of these families live in, they should, as a matter of fact, receive much more assistance from private and public agencies than they do. If one views the evils in the living conditions of the vast poorer section of Puerto Ricans in the United States, one incontestable fact stands out: the Puerto Ricans have not caused these evils. Their presence has merely highlighted already existing shortcomings. These evils are the result of neglect, greed, maladministration and prejudice.

The United States in general and New York City in particular have been geared to accept new populations. And larger numbers than Puerto Ricans constitute have been assimilated in the past. The key problem of Puerto Ricans is housing. New arrivals are forced to live in the most crowded, dilapidated and vermin-infested areas. They have to live in the worst possible accommodations, in special segregated or semi-segregated areas. When they live in other parts of a city they also have to live crowded together in small space. All this of course applies only to the poorer

Puerto Ricans. It has become customary for landlords to divide even small apartments into their single rooms and rent even the smallest rooms as separate apartments. Often they make an "apartment" out of the kitchen, too. It happens frequently that several families with children live in one such room. Social workers have described to me these conditions, with mattresses on the floor and cockroaches climbing on the walls. These rooms have, of course, neither bathroom nor kitchen. In this way landlords have made out of a building with only 60 apartments—240 apartments! And this happens even in sectors of the city where one would not expect it. One can get a picture of how bad some of these rooms are from a case reported by the Deputy Housing Commissioner of New York where in one building there were "24 Housing Department violations, in addition to Health Department violations." For one dilapidated room in this building Puerto Ricans had to pay fifteen dollars a week, *i.e.*, over sixty dollars a month. It certainly is adding insult to injury when it is said that Puerto Ricans choose of their own volition to live in such places.

The median rent for such a single room used as a dwelling-unit has been calculated to be sixty-three dollars a month (Sophia M. Robison. 1953). Actually even such a median figure does not give a correct picture, because it includes those who have to pay much more. Social workers have reported to me cases where Puerto Ricans had to pay for a deteriorated, very small room eighty dollars a month. There are also many cases where Puerto Ricans had to pay twenty-five dollars a week for a small room, which adds up to one hundred dollars a month. Sometimes so many sleep in one room that they have to sleep in shifts. In the summer you can see some people sitting on the steps in front of the houses who are there because others are sleeping in the space inside. The landlord may charge them by person instead of by room.

If you want to look behind the rosy scene painted by some public officials you can make your own investigation in a "hot bed" section. There are grocery stores open to the public into the early hours of the morning. Why do so many Puerto Ricans buy groceries there at two A.M.? For many of them the reason is that they live in a "hot bed." That means that the landlord has cut up the apartments into small rooms and rents a room for eight hours. After that time is up tenants have to go, leaving their things there, and someone else comes to sleep who in turn has to leave after his eight hours to make room for a third eight-hour tenant. They buy groceries for only one meal—at a time decided by which is their eight-hour shift—because it is not practicable to leave food when their time is up. Pushing my own investigations a little further, I found that the people who own these buildings with "hot beds" are not fly-by-night operators, but pillars of the community.

Many Puerto Rican families are constantly on the move. In a small way that is what happened to the Santana family. They can't complain about bad conditions, because if they do the landlord will put them out or—if they complain to an official agency—they run the risk that the building will be condemned and then they are evicted. Many are not acceptable for public housing, for one reason or another. They may live in common-law marriage because they did not have the eight dollars they needed in Puerto Rico to get married, or they do not have money enough for divorce, or the whereabouts of the husband may be unknown. All this is of course terribly hard on the children, who rank among the most deprived children in the United States. Many children come here to live with aunts, uncles, grandparents or other relatives, while one or both parents remain in Puerto Rico. It is impossible to measure the loneliness, insecurity and confusion suffered by these children.

The disruptive effect of the shocking housing conditions of the Puerto Ricans is now recognized by the school authorities. A little more than two weeks after the Santana case occurred the Board of Education issued a special order: "Experience indicates that new arrivals in New York City especially those from Puerto Rico frequently move several times the first year of residence in New York City. Furthermore because of the fact that they frequently move in with other families it is often difficult for the school to reach them by mail." The order goes on to suggest to school principals "the practice of inquiring each month" (!) where and with whom these children live.

What do children think about all this? In the fourth grade a teacher asked the children what they would wish for if their wish could be fulfilled by magic. One Puerto Rican pupil answered, "I would wish for nine beds, so that everybody in the family could have a bed."

There are various ways of looking at these objective

housing difficulties. A recent social report "The Puerto Rican Migration" by the directors of three neighborhood settlement centers states that Puerto Ricans have not received adequate basic education in using apartment facilities. It suggests as a cure that the Housing Authority should educate and supervise Puerto Rican families in apartment living! Puerto Rican families are forced to live in what a recent report of the New Jersey Department of Education described as "houses nobody should live in," in overcrowded single rooms, in unfit basements with puddles of water in them, taking turns in shifts in hot bed sections. To advocate "education in apartment living" as a cure for these evil conditions is a mockery of social welfare. If you provide people with a halfway decent apartment, you can show them in ten minutes how to live in it.

Housing and family life are closely interwoven. Puerto Rican women find employment more readily than the men, especially in the garment industry in jobs where the English language is not necessary. That affects the social and psychological state of the father and in turn affects the children. In general Puerto Ricans are pushed into the lowest jobs, are the last to be hired and the first to be fired. An easy current excuse for discrimination against Puerto Ricans in employment is the language difficulty. This however is not at all the real reason and it could be remedied by appropriate language courses. There are indeed employers who will not take Puerto Ricans because they don't speak English well enough; but there are others

who—at very small wages—will employ only Puerto
Ricans who cannot speak English!*

The fact that Puerto Ricans do not create deficien-
cies but merely highlight existing ones is especially
true of school education. The teacher has in fact been
dethroned and has to swallow all kinds of psychological theory thrust upon him by educational bureau-
crats who have little, if any, contact with children.
They talk about the whole child's adjustment and
consider it lowbrow if a teacher suggests that the best
way to help a child's adjustment in school is to teach
him elementary subjects well. A form letter currently
being sent to Puerto Rican parents in both English
and Spanish by a public school in the Bronx contains this dubious statement: "In the first year your
child will learn *more*, not less, by singing, dancing,
going on trips, and sharing with his many new
friends" (than by learning reading from a book, or
written arithmetic, or writing). Many of these chil-

---

* It is enlightening to note some of the English words that
have been taken over into the Spanish language by Puerto
Ricans in New York. Among "Neoyorquismos" (New York-
isms) are these (from a novel by Guillermo Cotto-Thorner):

bigchot (big shot)	*jolope* (holdup)
blofero (bluffer)	*liquiar* (leak)
broque (broke)	*raquet* (racket)
cuarto furnido (furnished room)	*rilif* (relief)
chipe (cheap)	*soportar* (support)
desposé (dispossess)	*tofe* (tough)

trobel (trouble)

dren are in classes or schools that are to all intents and purposes segregated, where material and instruction are on a far lower level than in the other schools. Every once in a while this is denied or whitewashed; but I have testified to the fact under oath as an expert psychiatric witness before a High Court.* This applies to Puerto Rican as well as Negro children. According to the New York University Research Center for Human Relations, for every dollar spent in elementary schools for every Puerto Rican (or Negro) child, on furniture and instructional equipment, $7.60 is spent for each "white" child.

When Santana was not permitted in high school to take the course he wanted, that was true of many other children, too. But Puerto Rican children are especially discriminated against. It is also in large part due to discrimination that they are found in vocational high schools oftener than in academic high schools. They are also much too readily put in retarded classes on the basis of misleading psychological group tests.

In a large printed and mimeographed material given out by the school authorities to teachers a condescending and discriminatory attitude is unmistakable. Is it really necessary to tell teachers: "Accept-

* Wertham, Fredric: *Psychological Effects of School Segregation.* American Journal of Psychotherapy, *61* (1). 1952. 94-103. and *Psychiatric Observations on Abolition of School Segregation.* Journal of Educational Sociology, *26* (7). 1953. March. Hill & Greenberg: *Citizen's Guide to De-Segregation.* Beacon Press. Boston. 1955. p. 98.

ance of the Puerto Rican child by teachers is of the utmost importance"? Or "Welcome the newcomer (Puerto Rican) in a friendly manner"? Should that not be taken for granted? Is it necessary in the registration form of the New York City Junior High School to ask *the child,* in English and in Spanish, "Do you receive aid from the Department of Welfare"? In these publications for teachers there is also a tendency to improvise special methods for teaching Puerto Rican children to learn reading and other subjects.

Yet with all the emphasis on general adjustment in lieu of sane instruction by well-tried pedagogical methods, the integration with social service, guidance and mental hygiene is extraordinarily inefficient. For example, the Junior High Schools give Puerto Rican parents a list of "Agencies Which Assist the Migrant Puerto Rican and His Family." This list mentions agencies where no practical aid can be obtained for a Puerto Rican, and completely omits any mention of mental hygiene clinics where many of these children like Frank Santana could get social service and other guidance.

The standard excuse for so much educational inadequacy and discrimination is the "language barrier" which is supposed to be the biggest hurdle for the Puerto Rican child. This language difficulty, however, is being exaggerated out of all proportion. Children can learn languages easily and rapidly. Puerto Rican children—although the opposite has been claimed—are no exception.

In the field of health the discrimination against Puerto Ricans—excepting those financially well off—

shows up especially. This is also denied, as a rule, or embellished or explained away. The facts are there, however. In a study of a Bronx school ("The School and Community Look at Their Children") prepared by New York school authorities, occurs this paragraph: "The influx of Porto (sic!) Ricans has a tendency to aggravate health problems in the neighborhood, because of the changes of climate, problems of adaptation to a new mode of living and the emotional tensions that complete change of environment coupled with low income bring." It isn't the number of Puerto Ricans that causes the health problem, but the neglect of public health and social service measures. And "emotional tensions" do not cause rat bites and rickets.

In large cities the disease tuberculosis is caused not only by the bacillus of tuberculosis, but by the bacillus of prejudice. In 1954 all other groups of the population showed a decrease in new cases of tuberculosis. The Puerto Ricans showed an increase. This had nothing to do with any increase in numbers, which is always used as a handy excuse, for in 1954 the migration of Puerto Ricans to New York was lower than in the eight previous years. (N.Y. Tuberculosis and Health Ass'n. 1955.) There is another unique circumstance about tuberculosis in the population of New York. Whereas generally the incidence of tuberculosis is much higher in men than in women, this ratio is reversed for Puerto Ricans. These high tuberculosis rates have nothing to do with any inherent biological vulnerability and the high rates for women have nothing to do with their sex. It is all a question of low economic status with all of its consequences, poor working conditions and nutrition, poor housing and lack of decent prophylactic and medical facilities. The increase of tuberculosis among persons of Puerto Rican origin is an indictment in itself:

1943—191 new cases
1950—574 new cases
1951—636 new cases
1952—718 new cases
1953—725 new cases
1954—783 new cases

Rickets in children has almost disappeared from the general population in this country. Now cases are coming up among Puerto Rican children. The full extent of the incidence of rickets among Puerto Ricans is not known because they do not receive enough medical attention in general and cases are only belatedly diagnosed. We know now that rickets is a completely preventable disease, so that the almost unique incidence among Puerto Rican children speaks for itself. Infant mortality among Puerto Ricans is very high. In 1951 it was 30 per 1,000 live births. (Weiner. 1954.)

Although the outward appearance may be deceiving, a disproportionate number of Puerto Rican children suffer from malnutrition and avitaminosis. This is grossly neglected, and not taken sufficiently into account when their school behavior is evaluated. Their teeth are often in very bad condition and even physicians or teachers who notice that can do little about it. There are good facilities for dental care for children from low-income families. Unfortunately they have the policy that families on relief are not eligible, and this affects the poorest Puerto Rican children. A disease that affects Puerto Rican children on account of their living in unsuitable quarters is lead poisoning. This may lead to brain deterioration (lead encephalopathy). Of course other children get that too; but it has been determined that the Puerto Rican population, on account of its poverty, is most exposed. Naturally this wouldn't happen if cheap paints with a heavy lead content were labelled POISON. Another example of health problems is rat bites of children. It is not unusual for those who really examine these children to find evidence of rat bites on foreheads.

For years in New York some city hospitals have been overcrowded. I have often seen severely ill patients on cots or in corridors. But a high city official stated publicly that "the influx of Puerto Ricans has overcrowded the hospitals." *Influx* seems to be a favorite word to use for Puerto Ricans who rightfully and hopefully come to this country. They never just come to this country. They always have "swarmed in" or "rushed in" or "poured in." If hospitals are overcrowded it is not because there are so many Puerto Ricans but because there are so many people who are sick.

In the mental health field, prejudice and discrimination against Puerto Ricans, especially Puerto Rican youths, is pronounced. It is years now since I drew public attention in lectures to the fact that Puerto

Rican young people are much too frequently committed to institutions. I especially referred to institutions for mental defectives and to reformatories. This continues to the present day.

In courts, Puerto Ricans who have not yet mastered the English language well are often unfairly treated. In the Special Sessions and Magistrates Courts of New York the official interpreters often translate badly. They give a *literal* translation; that is they translate the words rather than the sense. In a court of justice that may give a very wrong impression.

The idea that Puerto Ricans are intellectually and emotionally different from and inferior to others, and consequently dangerous, is common. It does not exist only in the general population. I have encountered it again and again among professional workers: doctors, psychiatrists, psychoanalysts, psychologists, lawyers, clergymen, social workers, teachers. Sometimes this prejudice is more or less unconscious, but often it is openly expressed. Long before the big migration of Puerto Ricans to the continental United States a pseudo-scientific mantle was thrown over prejudice against them. A Special Committee of the Chamber of Commerce of the City of New York sponsored a psychological investigation, "Reactions of Puerto Rican Children in New York City to Psychological Tests." This investigation was carried out by three psychologists on 240 Puerto Rican children. It reached the conclusion that Puerto Rican children have "a marked and serious inferiority in native ability"; that "Puerto Ricans are adding greatly to the already tremendous problem of intellectually sub-normal school retardates of alien parentage, whence are recruited most delinquents and criminals"; finally, that "most Puerto Rican children cannot be assimilated in the existing type of civilization and they are helping to turn the tide back to a lower stage of progress." The Special Committee of the Chamber of Commerce adds: ". . . inasmuch as a grant of Statehood can never be rescinded, the investigation certainly suggests that the proposition to incorporate Puerto Rico as a State in the Federal Union should be held in abeyance."

This of course was not science. There were many obvious faults in the methods of investigation, and no conclusions of this type can be drawn from ordinary group psychological tests. But even at this moment Puerto Rican children are being falsely evaluated on the basis of just such tests. This does great harm to the learning career of the individual child. It impairs his motivation for learning.

When Puerto Ricans get emotionally disturbed as a result of their hard-pressed circumstances, they are apt to be wrongly diagnosed. Language difficulty may add to wrong interpretations. So it happens that Puerto Rican adolescents are incorrectly diagnosed as schizophrenic and committed to state hospitals or called mentally defective and sent to institutions for the defective. Even judicial notice has been taken of such falsely committed cases. But the situation has not improved. If I were to believe only half of what ex-patients have told me, conditions in some of these institutions are truly barbaric. Owing to general prejudice, Puerto Ricans get the worst of these shocking abuses. It is a coincidence that the attorneys for Santana, as I am writing this, have brought to light conditions in a state institution for mental defectives in which there are over five hundred Puerto Ricans among forty-three hundred inmates. For all this number there is only one psychologist. So when Puerto Ricans are committed there on the basis of false test results, owing to language difficulties and other factors, it takes quite a while before such mistakes are discovered—if they are found out at all. It was testified to that there was a great deal of beating, cruelly prolonged use of restraint sheets, protracted solitary confinement and other inhuman practices.

The Puerto Rican coming from the Island to the continental United States has to face one entirely new fact which is almost beyond his comprehension—race prejudice, especially in its most naked form, race prejudice based on color. This is a sensitive subject of great dynamic importance. It plays havoc with their adjustment. While in Puerto Rico discrimination on account of color does not exist*, the Puerto Rican in the United States sooner or later discovers that sharp distinctions are made here between Puerto Ricans who are considered "white" and those who are "dark-complexioned and Negro." The distinction as to

* Recently color prejudice has been imported into the Island from the mainland. In the best new hotels, e.g., the Caribe Hilton, Negroes are permitted to stay, but may not sun themselves on the hotel's beaches nor swim in the hotel's ocean. (Hanson. 1955.)

whether a Puerto Rican belongs to one group or the other is often entirely arbitrary, but nonetheless has serious consequences for him. Even in social science studies a distinction has actually been made between "dark-skinned," "white" and "intermediate" within the Puerto Rican group. (Robison. 1954.)

Why is this color prejudice so important? New York City Councilman Earl Brown has given the answer: "Nowhere in America does the Negro enjoy freedom equal to that of the white man." And he defines freedom: "Knowing that you have the respect of other men," as "human dignity" and "the right of the individual to speak up for his and for others' rights."

It is an official policy among some public and private social agencies that application sheets have an item: *Color,* to be filled out as "P.R." indicating Puerto Ricans. *Nationality* is filled out as "U.S." This is a common social service practice. In scientific psychiatric papers I have seen patients designated as "of Spanish-Puerto Rican stock," which indicates that they are regarded as white. This is of importance because dark-complexioned Puerto Ricans, like Negroes, are not admitted to many private and university psychiatric hospitals.

The effects of this color prejudice have been far-reaching. In an article series in the Amsterdam *News* it was pointed out that "along with the United States education of the Puerto Rican goes education for race prejudice and they are becoming increasingly aware of the benefits of 'being white' and tend to withdraw more and more from darker persons, even members of their own group." Children of course are particularly harmed by this. It is hypocritical to deplore juvenile gang warfare while color prejudice enters into all their human relations. It has actually come about that darker-complexioned Puerto Rican children don't want to learn English for fear they will be mistaken for Negroes. Santana knew of instances where a boy who was too friendly with Puerto Ricans or Negroes was beaten up for it. A fourteen-year-old delinquent boy who had been involved in gang fights against Negroes and Puerto Ricans told me in a group therapy session: "If a Puerto Rican's skin is a little dark, if he speaks English, I consider him a colored person. If he speaks Spanish I consider him white. That's what a lot of people think. I thought that myself; but I don't think it is right any more."

The harmful influence of all this on Puerto Rican children is very great. And nothing can be done about it if it is disguised by such glib talk as "ethnic clashes with all their background of varying cultural patterns." I know instances where children refused to sit next to dark-complexioned Puerto Ricans in school. That has nothing to do with "cultural patterns."

Mr. Joseph Montserrat, director of the New York City Office of the Commonwealth of Puerto Rico, has vividly described how at the age of nine or ten he was first called a derogatory term applying to Puerto Ricans. "It made me feel that I was not just a human being, but a peculiar type of inferior human being." Prejudice against Puerto Ricans is specifically taught to children as entertainment. A story in one comic book, a creep, uses the most derogatory epithets for Puerto Ricans twelve times: "greasy—," "dirty—," etc. It draws attention to dark skin color and black hair. It adds a dash of religious prejudice by speaking of a "Spanish Catholic family," and an "unfamiliar religion." The story is about a Puerto Rican boy who falls in love with a very blonde not-Puerto Rican girl. The girl's father and some neighbors kidnap him in the dark of night, tie his hands behind his back, put a sack over his head and beat him to death. In the last picture is the sickly hypocritical "moral": it wasn't the boy, but the girl, who was in the sack and got beaten to death.

Even in a regular children's book dealing with Puerto Ricans, prejudice creeps in—although the author evidently does not intend it to be there. It is precisely this unconscious kind of prejudice that poisons children's minds, however. In the second paragraph of this book you hear that Puerto Ricans drop garbage out of their windows. Color of skin, eyes and hair are used as the salient characteristics of everybody, from the cliché "olive-skinned" to those "with darker skin and the flashing smiles of Negroes," these being contrasted with the blonde and blue- (or gray-) eyed others. The smallness of Puerto Ricans is especially pointed out, too. As for history, children are told that Puerto Rico was "adopted by the United States almost by accident." Shades of General Miles! This kind of book, whatever its intent, gives non-Puerto Rican children a stereotyped idea about Puerto Ricans, and Puerto Rican children a self-depreciative image of themselves.

A few days after I finished my examination of Santana, at one of the many meetings where delinquency is discussed a civic leader propounded that "juvenile delinquency generates an atmosphere of tension" and that it "frequently manifests itself along racial lines thereby infecting entire neighborhoods." What happens is just the other way around. The delinquency does not generate the tension, the tension generates the delinquency. And children do not infect neighborhoods with race prejudice; the neighborhoods infect the children with it.

I asked the owner of a large fruit farm in Pennsylvania who for years has employed Puerto Ricans, what his opinion of them was. To run such a farm as successfully as he does, you must know people as well as fruit. He was not exposed to all the patter about ethnic groups, subcultures and basic personality types and structures. He knew facts. "I tell you how they are," he told me. "They are just as we are. Maybe they are a little brighter. If you tell them something they listen. Some of our young people don't."

VII   *Reversal*

"The truth, if it is subordinated to an error, becomes an untruth."

—von Ranke

I had to talk to Santana about the events that led to his arrest and imprisonment. To the extent that one could apply that adjective to him at all, he seemed eager to tell me. He said that he had not joined a gang, but had helped to found a club, a stick-ball club. It was called the Navahos from the beginning. That was in February, 1955. "We started a stick-ball club—about ten boys. We were all Puerto Ricans. Some were born here."

This club had nothing to do with gang activities when it was founded. The members got themselves jerseys with the club name on them. Each jersey cost seven dollars, which they paid themselves from smaller sums they saved up. Santana took from his wallet a bill which he showed me. The bill was made out to Frank Santana by an athletic supply company. It gives all the specifications for the jerseys: *style:* gaucho; *color:* black; gold band at the bottom and at the collar; *Navahos* on the back; etc. The bill has the nicknames of eight boys, with Taza's name first. Three dollars was paid on account, according to this bill. Then on the back is a careful accounting of small amounts of money received from the different boys. On March third it is receipted as "Paid in Full."

To show me that this was all open and that there was no secretive gang business, he showed me a photograph of five boys, including himself. The group is posed in front of some house steps and one boy is holding up a jersey like a pennant, showing the name *Navahos*. Frank told me the names of the boys in the picture. "They are all Spanish guys." He explained that this group was just started for sports.

"What's the difference," I asked him, "between a stick-ball club and a gang?"

"The boys want to have a gang," he said, "because there are so many gangs around. Gangs are for protection. We became a gang."

It seemed clear to me that these boys formed a sports group composed of "Spanish guys" because they couldn't join other groups anyhow. The gang character of the group developed as a reaction to the mores of the streets in the neighborhood. It wasn't a "hostile boy" joining a gang or becoming a "gangster." It was the response of a boy trying to get together with others and conforming to hostile signals from outside.

I never like to ask a prisoner about a gun. However carefully or tactfully you approach the subject, you at once cease to be a psychiatrist and become a detective to the person whom you question. But from past experiences I knew that I would be asked about the gun in court. In my mind's eye I could see the district attorney shaking his finger at my nose and saying with some emphasis, "So! You didn't ask him about the gun! *That* was of no importance for your psychiatric opinion? You only want to know if he draws figures with hands or not!"

So I said something about the gun. "It was a Beretta," he said right off, with no hesitation whatever. "A .38 automatic Italian Beretta gun." I asked him to write down the name *Beretta* and he did. I am not an expert on guns. Nor is he. But the Beretta at once established a sort of communion between us, for we both learned about Berettas from the same source, children's comic books. In millions of them there are pages describing this gun in glamorous terms. And the comic-book editor especially asks on an editorial page:

> How about the Page Showing the Pistols?
> Does it interest you?

The page about the Beretta gun goes like this:

> The story behind the Italian *BERETTA* is one of achievement in the face of defeat. In the year 1934 Mussolini and the Italian army were convincing themselves of their invincibility when they introduced the surprisingly fine semi-automatic Beretta pistols. Even guns are born of necessity and the Beretta is no exception. Being an easy weapon to conceal, it could be easily strapped to an Italian officer's leg, under the trousers, for use in the event of capture. During World War II the German army purchased the Italian Beretta to augment their already famous Luger pistol. . . .

And of course there are illustrations of the glamorous Beretta gun and its uses. Browning said:

> We're made so that we love
> First when we see them painted, things we
> have passed.

One might paraphrase that:

We're made so that we are tempted
First when we see them painted, by things
we have passed.

"Frank," I said, "it would help me if I could understand why you got the gun in the first place. You don't
have to tell me if you don't want to; but don't tell me
anything wrong."

"I told the police I had the gun a long time. The
same day, I got it. I told the police one way and they
wanted me to say the other way, the way they wanted
it. They didn't beat me. They beat Superman and——
(another boy)."

"What I would like to understand, Frank, is what
you got the gun *for?*"

"To defend myself."

"Do you really need a gun for that?"

"I'm not goin' with nothin' when they're tryin' to
get me. Same week, walking on the street alone, one
Golden Guineas with a yellow and black jersey came
to me and wanted to fight. We have the same-colored
jersey they have. I said, 'I don't want to fight you.'
Two more came. They said, 'Why don't you want to
fight? Are you *yellow?*' I said, 'No, I'm not yellow. I'm
boxing.' Then the three say, 'We rip the jersey off
you!' Then I say, 'Go ahead! Rip it off!' Then they
said, 'We're goin' to *get* you!' He was goin' to the
same school my girl goes to."

This was a familiar kind of threat. In the Hooky
Club (made up of delinquent children with whom I
did group therapy), adolescents often talked about
this kind of thing. Fifteen or twenty years ago this

would not have been serious. A boy got threatened—
even beaten, by others, or joined with others in beating another boy. But nowadays (although many people writing and talking about child guidance do not
seem to know it) children get viciously beaten
by other children. They even are tortured or killed.
Such violence (although it is convenient to say it was
"always so") is something entirely new. And a Puerto
Rican boy threatened by other boys can well have a
realistic fear, not only of being beaten but of being
seriously hurt. The whole subject of Puerto Rican
youths as victims of attacks has been kept quiet. Frequently these attacks are not cleared up and the at-
tackers are not traced. I recall the case of a fifteen-
year-old boy: walking with a girl of the same age, in
the evening, he was stopped by five boys and knocked
to the pavement. As he tried to get up he was shot in
the back three times, and killed.

The day when the Golden Guineas threatened Santana was Thursday the twenty-eighth of April. Saturday the thirtieth, two days later, was the fateful day.
He told me that on that Saturday evening Superman
(head of the gang) was carrying his (Frank's) gun.
Superman is fifteen years old.

"Tell me about what happened that Saturday evening."

"Superman and——, he's a colored guy, and I
walked on Wilson and Burke Avenue near Two Hundred and Ninth Street. I live at One Hundred and
Fifty-sixth Street. Blankenship came over to us——"

I interrupted him. "Look, Frank. You don't have to
tell me anything about this trouble itself. I only want

to know what kind of a boy you are, not what you've done. That's up to the legal people. So if you don't answer me about that I shan't mind. But if you tell me something that isn't true, you confuse me, and that makes it more difficult for me to help you."

He did not seem much interested in the details of what I was saying. He just repeated, "He came over to us."

I interrupted him again. "Frank, I've shown you some of these clippings. I have many more. The best papers not only in this city but all over the country, the radio, television——they all know that Blankenship was going to a movie and that *you* went up to *him* and stopped him. They even told about that from the pulpit. Everybody knows it. So why do you tell me something different?"

There was no pause when I stopped talking. He just repeated what he had said and went on. "He came over to us. He said, 'Who is the leader?' Superman said, 'I am the leader.' Blankenship pushed him. Superman pulled a gun out. Blankenship said, 'Don't point that gun on me!' Then——"

"Wait a minute, Frank," I said. "You say that Blankenship first pushed Superman. That *he* started laying his hands on you Navahos?"

"He pushed him."

I interrupted again, quietly. "Frank, we're getting this all in reverse. If that were true, somebody else would know it and the papers would have printed it. Please don't tell it to me the wrong way. If you're going to do that, we'd better talk about something else."

He was as polite and calm as ever, but he just repeated what he had said: "Blankenship pushed him. Superman pulled a gun out. And Blankenship said, 'Don't point that gun on me!' So Superman put it away under his belt. Blankenship turned around. Some more boys came. Blankenship talked to Pedro. He pushed Pedro. Pedro says, 'Yes, we are the Enchanters.' Blankenship said, 'I'm in the Red Wings. We——' "

"Now, Frank!" I interrupted again. "Look. Did I understand that correctly? Did you say that Blankenship said he was a member of a gang?"

"He said, 'I'm in the Red Wings.' "

The sun burned through the jail window into the little room, and I suddenly realized that this was a hot day.

"Frank," I said, "this is getting serious. You understand that the police and the district attorney have investigated your case. All the papers and all the best radio and television commentators have said over and over again that Blankenship was a model boy and had nothing whatever to do with gangs. Now if he *were* in a gang, some reporter would have found it out! And the district attorney would have corrected the story that was around, and that has influenced everybody so much. Maybe you misunderstood what Blankenship said. Maybe he said he'd call the Red Wings, or something like that?"

He remained polite and unruffled. "Blankenship said, 'I'm in the Red Wings. We're a brother club with the Golden Guineas.' I took the gun from Superman.

When I pulled it out, all of a sudden it went off. Blankenship is much bigger than I. Six feet, it said in the paper."

All the essential points about the circumstances of the shooting that he gave me were confirmed and corroborated later. It was like the reversal in an old Greek tragedy which leads to sudden recognition. This was not a wanton, deliberate, first-degree homicide. It was the now-all-too-common juvenile fracas, with its horrible, almost casual violence.

Even before any shot was fired or any trigger pulled, this was a situation fraught with violence. What is the reason for this violence?

We make it too easy for ourselves if we separate this problem from what adults do. Why is it made so easy for juveniles to buy narcotics? To my knowledge, they were even sold to kids on the grounds of a psychiatric hospital for juvenile drug addicts! Adolescents have boasted to me that they can get me heroin within an hour. Why is it made so easy for them to buy guns of every description, so easy that home-made zip guns have now gone out of fashion? As for knives—the widest variety of them is advertised and sold directly to children.

Much of what is said about the violence of juvenile gangs, especially officially, is somewhat removed from the living reality. In an official directive to the personnel of a junior high school the causes of conflicts among gangs are enumerated; but one of the most potent and dynamic causes is left out. This is race-nationality prejudice and antagonism, which is a direct reflection of adult life, adult values and adult tensions.

When these juveniles war on the same people whom their elders express prejudice against, they feel consciously or unconsciously that they are acting with the adults' approval and according to the mores of the community.

Almost a year before the Santana case the newspapers carried reports of violence including murder committed by members of the Red Wings. One paper stated: "The Red Wings fought against the incursion of the Puerto Ricans in the neighborhood. . . . As the Puerto Rican population increased there were bitter battles with the Red Wings."

A year and a half before the Santana case a school official stated: "The Red Wings have only one activity, and that is beating up Puerto Ricans. They are from fifteen to eighteen years old. They have no meeting place. Beating up Puerto Ricans is the only thing they have in common."

About six months before the Santana case a fourteen-year-old patient said about swimming pools in public parks in New York: "These swimming pools cannot be used by any Puerto Rican kid. That's the unwritten law. The little Spanish kids get ducked until they almost die. Only the Red Wings go there. Any other kid has to fear for his life if he dares to go there. Occasionally they may permit a Negro to use the pool —if they know the Negro. The Italians have become more friendly towards the American Negroes since the Puerto Ricans moved in." This refers to public parks, and to swimming pools ostensibly under the control and supervision of adults!

I know whole city blocks where, if a boy does not

belong to a gang, the presumption is that there may be something wrong with him. What happens to a boy in such a section who does not join a gang is illustrated by a fourteen-year-old Puerto Rican boy. He stayed away from school because he was afraid. (And typical of the mix-up about Puerto Rican pupils in the school system is the fact that for years there he was registered under the wrong name.) In the first schools he went to, "the Negroes beat me"; in the next school "the Italians beat me. They threatened me with a knife and punched me. It's not only me, they do it to the other Spanish boys, too. I have friends but they don't back me up. They are afraid. They are Spanish. It's a tough city."

Santana's stick-ball club was a sports group. It became connected with the Navahos street gang. I found out later from young ex-members how the Navahos street gang originally came into being. There was a group of young Puerto Rican boys who often were "hanging around near the Spanish theatre." Every once in a while the Golden Guineas came around and pushed a boy and threatened or beat him. It is out of these beginnings that the Navahos originally organized their street gang.

We know enough about the origins of violence, the genesis of gangs and the development of delinquency to do something about it in a sound way. It is not only a matter of curbing children, but one of restraining adults. A false understanding of democracy is one of the obstacles. At the time of the Santana case (May, 1955) the American Civil Liberties Union got out a pamphlet with a spirited defense of rights—the rights of the comic-book publishers. It says that there may be "some risk that some persons along the line may possibly get hurt"; that "our life is founded upon risk" and that "risk is an indelible mark of democracy." Risk was the hallmark of Nietzsche's philosophy, and of Hitler's and Mussolini's state. What democracy is based on is not risk, but security.

Only the smallest part of what we know about delinquency is put into practise. A good deal of what is being done is a matter of improvisation. The New York City Youth Board's much-publicized "street club workers" are typical. They use what is officially called "the hanging around method." This means that they hang around street corners and candy stores trying to join youths' activities, such as crap games. Their role is ambiguous, half-secretive and amateurish. They practice a kind of social work without social work, detective work without detecting, psychotherapy without psychotherapy. They play amateur psychoanalyst and speak of "sick boys" or boys who are just "compensating," and make statements like "Many kids come with no anxiety; we sometimes have to provoke it" (sic!). In an uncontrolled situation that can, of course, do only harm. Their approach to such serious problems as guns and violence is amiable and casual, like this: "Look, fellas," a street club worker actually told a group of boys, "I don't know, but if you got a piece (gun) there, get rid of it before you get in trouble! I don't know why I bother with you crazy guys anyway." Such patter is not what the boys need. The whole approach is unscientific. It romanticizes both delinquency prevention and delinquency. Recently this is how such work has been described: "Street club workers are taking their lives in their hands and working for as long as 30 hours at a stretch in the rain and snow, in the day and night, striving to open the minds of this city's kids to a glimmer of humane values." This is not how a large city should help its children and prevent violence. When we *create* means of violence such as the atom bomb, we do not go about it in any such sentimental-heroic and essentially futile way. We use science and do not leave it to young men groping at night in rain and snow.

The seeds of violence are manifold. We must know the development of a boy's personality and the connections between the delinquent act and the boy's actual experiences, thoughts and complexes. But a child is more than a bundle of symptom-formations. It is not accidental that children, even very young children, nowadays commit such violent acts. But we can only understand that if we include the impersonal sources of violence. We can very well take both into account— the basic internal needs of the individual youth and his objective social environment. This environment includes not only the narrow circle of the family but also social economic conditions in the widest sense. The connections between the wages of a needle worker in Puerto Rico and a gun in the hands of a boy on the sidewalks of New York may not be apparent; but they do exist. A continuous process of interaction takes place between the individual and his social environment.

What is actually taught to those who have to work professionally with delinquents and pre-delinquents

is very different. For example, a psychiatrist of a big
social agency has demanded that we study the unconscious development of each individual gang member.
If people are made to feel that this is what is needed,
they are persuaded that the necessary measures of
guidance and protection are wasted effort. Even if the
unconscious development of every Navaho, Golden
Guinea and Red Wing were to be studied, the dynamic setting of this gang violence would still elude
us.

Delinquency in the last analysis stems not from the
fact that children neglect their duties, but from
the fact that we violate their rights. Children do have
three fundamental rights: the right to health, to education and to protection. In each great epoch the
rights of children, who make up the most vulnerable
segment of the population, have had to be proclaimed.
Christianity announced: "Suffer little children to
come unto Me." During the industrial revolution children's rights against the abuses of child labor had to
be protected by law. Freud proclaimed the right of
children to acknowledgment of their instinctual life
and its vicissitudes. At present the enormous development of mass media has created a new situation. As
a psychiatrist told the Northern California Mental
Health Conference, "I think you all must share the
anxiety and fearfulness of parents in the endless struggle to counteract the lurid comics, the foolish movies,
the blaring TV, . . . with some technique other than
force or cunning." Only two fifths of the adult population of the United States has access to library books;
but almost one hundred per cent of the child popula-

tion has direct access to crime comic books. From movies, radio, television and comics, children are exposed to the excitement of violence. They need protection from the adult world which is still so far from having solved its own problem of mass violence.

Sitting in the little room in the Bronx County Jail, trying to figure out why a youth kills, I thought of Auden's verse:

> The situation of our time
> Surrounds us like a baffling crime.

Atomic bombs have a physical radioactive fallout. The immense harm which that can do is being recognized and widely discussed. They also have a psychological fallout, however, and that is *not* widely recognized. It poisons this generation and—like the physical radioactive particles—affects the next one. The human mind in its technological advance has created the atom bomb. But the atom bomb has also had an effect on the human mind. Many delinquents are not "bad"; they are poisoned. If we follow all the clues, the circle of guilt enlarges in every case. No single focus within the individual or family is enough. We must view the individual also in the wider perspective of his historical existence. Otherwise we lose sight of a part of his individuality and cannot give him real help.

A case like Santana's is a reflection on our whole educational system. Formerly children were taught not to point with their finger at anybody. Nowadays, wherever you go, children point at you *with guns*— and parents and teachers think it is cute! In mass media violence is used to maintain the child's interest. Why should a boy like Santana be allowed to play truant for so long? Why should his mind be led to gangs and guns and violent self-protection? At his age a boy should have serious vocational and cultural interests. He was intellectually well enough equipped for that.

The difficult task required of us is to see the beam in our own eye. Do we have enough faith in the educability of children? Is our social life so ordered that we can educate them in non-violence, give them psychological protection and guidance, and supply them with models and discipline that lead to self-control? We know enough about delinquency to act, to treat and to prevent cases like Santana's.

There is only one complication. Do we really *want* to stop delinquency? That idea preoccupied me a great deal, the more I learned about the Santana case. It led me to indulge in a fantasy.

VIII   *Strike*   A Fantasy

"There we get down to a definition of terms again. What is crime and violence?"

—Senator at Hearing of Senate Subcommittee to Investigate Juvenile Delinquency

It all started when I got a letter from a boy in high school. His letter went like this:

Dear Dr. Wertham:
I read a few days ago in the *Herald Tribune* that the Court signed an order for you to examine Frank Santana in jail. I suppose you have seen other cases like that. We are supposed to write a class paper on "What Adults Do To Combat Juvenile Delinquency." Can you tell me how I can find out and where I should read about it?
Thank you.
(signed) —— —— ——

I read that letter late one night, tired after a long day's work. It started me thinking. Supposing the children really looked for facts, what would they find?

Many years of work with children and their parents have given me a pretty good idea of what is actually done—or rather not done—to help children. The discrepancy between pronouncements and deeds is an abyss. We keep asking for more and more money for investigations and research, meanwhile leaving the youngsters to shift for themselves. What would happen, I wondered, if they took things into their own hands?

That set me to picturing the possibilities. I fancied the boy discovering the vacuum that was behind all the promises and appropriations. In my fantasy he talks it over with another boy.

"You know," says the other boy. "I don't think society gives a rap about what happens to us kids any-

how. When we do something wrong they lock us up—
or if they feel good they may let us go. But they never
listen to our side. We wouldn't even dare to tell it to
them."

"I got an idea!" says the first boy. "Let's *stop* the
whole thing. The whole delinquency business. *Let's go
on strike!*"

The idea spread like a forest fire. During recess
these two boys told their idea to others in their class
and it went all over the school in no time. During the
weekend several boys hitchhiked to other cities to
spread the news: Delinquency is out!

When youngsters want to do something they *really*
want to do it. They are not like grownups who make
compromises at every step. Before they know it (the
grownups, I mean), they don't do what they set out to
do at all, but are content to talk about a lot of abstract
things and let it rest at that. The children did not
bother about definitions of juvenile delinquency. They
didn't ask what is crime, what is violence. They knew
what they were not supposed to do and they proceeded from that. They also knew that it was very easy
to become delinquent. They figured it would be simple for the older kids to help the younger ones. They
didn't know that it "takes years and years of research
to understand juvenile delinquency," and that delinquency is "an extremely complex problem," and that
to do something about it one must "plumb the most
hidden recesses of human motives." They were so un-
sophisticated that they thought you just had to stop it.

Children are naïve and do not try to get some advantage for themselves out of everything as grownups

do. For example, they don't make nearly so much
money out of committing delinquency as the adults
make out of combatting it. They do not go in for so
much self-deception, either.

The great question was whether they should tell
the grownups about their delinquency strike. Some
youngsters tried, in a tentative sort of way, to mention
something about it; but it didn't work. What they were
doing was against all the theories. So they had to keep
it secret, even from their own parents, because they
were afraid their parents wouldn't understand and
wouldn't trust them.

Youngsters have one-track minds. If the strike was
to be against delinquency, then it was also a strike
against all the grownups who provoked them into it.
The worst delinquency was violence and murder. But
they saw it as entertainment in the mass media everywhere around them, even though the older kids knew
so well that it wasn't good for the younger ones. They
couldn't make the fine distinctions between different
degrees of evils that we make: between toy guns
that look exactly like the real thing and can be used in
hold-ups, and real guns; between television programs
with many murders and those with only one or two;
between stories describing drug addiction and rape in
detail and these acts themselves; between comic books
describing crime and violence and comic books showing violence and cruelty to animals and by animals; between movies with brutality and murder in which the
actors wear big Western hats and other movies where
they have ordinary headgear.

So they had a lot to do. They boycotted all these

things, and just stopped giving adults money for them. The gun had been the commonest toy of American children, but that was all changed now. Where formerly almost every little boy and even many girls had been goaded by grown-up advertising into carrying one or even two guns, they now gave up guns. In one junior high school they collected signatures for a letter to President Eisenhower to protest against his having given a toy gun as a present to his little grandson, as the newspapers had widely reported, because it set a bad example, they thought. But the teacher got wind of this and persuaded them not to mail the letter. The teacher feared that the idea might be construed as subversive.

They knew that violence was bad. So they included that in their strike, wherever they found it. You can't really blame them, for they did not know all those refined arguments with which experts defend the sale of violence. The children did not know that it is the child that brings violence to the movie, for instance. They had not read that, as a psychiatric journal reported: "A Harvard group of researchers reported that the psychological disposition to violence, aggression or hostility which is already present in the individual plays a conditioning role in the effect of violence in the movies." They naïvely thought that it was the movies which were conditioning the children, and not the other way around. They did not talk glibly about "calculated risks," either; they just didn't want to take chances. So they boycotted all the movies-with-murder.

When a neighborhood movie, during its childrens'

Saturday matinee, had a double feature showing pretty rough stuff, they didn't wait for what would happen the following week. They just boycotted that theater right off, for good. Another problem for them was comic books. It was easy just not to buy them any more. But what to do with the old ones? You couldn't burn them, because the adults don't know the difference between books and comic books, and they'd call that book-burning. So the children hit upon a good solution: they gave all their comic books to grownups for *them* to read. As one boy put it, "They *make* them. Let them *read* them!"

Naturally in the process of getting their strike under way there were some difficulties. The boys and girls had to meet secretly to discuss their plans. At one meeting in an abandoned basement one boy tried to defend Western movies. He was talked down. One girl got up and said, "My brother was on a ranch all last summer, and he says cowboys *never* have guns! They don't have them and they don't use them. What's in the Westerns is all old stuff or lies!" So they decided to boycott all violent Western movies. Somehow word of this meeting got out to grownups. A few weeks later an FBI man visited the girl's home to question her parents. "We have information," he said, "that you are pacifists. What have you got against the draft?" It was finally straightened out when the girl explained that she had only talked about movies.

All over the country children met in what were formerly headquarters of juvenile gangs. They planned their strike strategy. Although they did not use the term, what they were doing was really *mental hygiene*. That was again the opposite of what is done by the grownups, who talk so much about mental hygiene but do not practice it for children. The adolescents agreed that the younger children need a lot of protection. Immature and uninformed as they were, they were unaware that a well-known book "Psychoanalysis and Kindergarten" had propounded to adults that "acts of brutality in play which are directed against a doll or a toy animal are best ignored." The adolescents felt that this was poor pedagogy and that they should explain to their younger brothers and sisters that one should be kind and considerate even to dolls and toy animals, regardless of grownups' strange theories.

At some meetings they decided to send letters to some grownups. In New Jersey, for example, they sent a letter to Mr. Steve Omert, member of the City Council and Chairman of the Police Committee in Raritan, New Jersey:

> Dear Mr. Omert:
>
> We have read in the paper that you made new rules for the police in your town. First rule: "Policemen must stop reading comic books while on duty."
>
> Second rule: "No comic books may be kept at police headquarters."
>
> We think this is a very good idea of yours. If comic-book reading is bad for children it is probably bad for policemen, too. It makes them too violent.
>
> (Signed)—Delinquency Strike Committee

In New York City the children sent a letter to the psychiatrist who was Director of the Mental Health service of the Childrens' Court who was caught stealing antiques for his office from a home in the country and was found guilty of petit larceny. That letter was brief:

> Dear Doctor:
> We know how you feel. Don't be upset. Why don't you join us?
> (Signed)—Delinquency Strike Committee

At first there were only rumors that such a strike was preparing and getting under way. Nobody believed them. Finally, however, the truth came out. All over the country the children had stopped being delinquent. And the results were disastrous.

The dirtiest trick the children did was to give up all truancy. All of them went to school, all the time. It created havoc. There were not enough classrooms, not enough schools, there were not enough teachers. The already overcrowded classes became even more overcrowded. Nobody knew *what* to do with the problem of increased school attendance. (The children knew truancy and delinquency are often related, and they weren't going to wait for adults to make more statistics about it.)

The economic consequences of the strike were calamitous. Nobody had realized that juvenile delinquency was so necessary for the economic well-being of so many people. The flourishing trade in (real) guns for minors was wiped out. The drug peddlers who hang around schools lost all their customers. The trade in pornography was affected severely. Children refused to buy dirty pictures any more, and adults lost this part of their business. Most of the more than three hundred toy-gun manufacturers went bankrupt. Even the air- and BB-gun industry was shaken, for children knew how much harm these guns can do and refused to buy them or accept them as gifts any longer. That in turn affected many magazines where these guns were glowingly advertised.

There was a panic in the fund-raising business. *Juvenile delinquency* had been a magic word for fund-raising purposes. Whether they had anything to do with delinquent children or not, philanthropic organizations found reference to juvenile delinquency very useful in their appeals for funds. In some of these non-profit organizations 35 per cent or 50 per cent or even more of the money goes for expenses and salaries in the organization. The delinquency strike cut deeply into these remunerative activities. The advertising business was in a turmoil. Children refused to buy any products from firms who sponsor violent television programs: Western, Superman, space or jungle. Breakfast food, candy and other manufacturers were seriously hit by this.

Children know no moderation, either. They boycotted also all products advertised directly to them. They felt advertising should be directed to the grownups and was no business for children. That affected the vitamin-manufacturing business, too, among others. The older children told the younger ones not to take the vitamin tablets so persuasively advertised by the "Ding Dong School" *directly to youngsters* of kindergarten and pre-kindergarten age! Some high-school girls wrote a letter about this to Jack Gould, the TV critic of *The New York Times*. It went like this:

Dear Mr. Gould:

We members of the Regional Delinquency Strike Committee congratulate you on your wonderful article "Peril in Small Pills" in the *Times*. You need not be concerned any more about this. We are telling our younger brothers and sisters to stay away from all pills advertised to them, and to leave it to their parents what is good for their health.

The movie industry was severely hit when the young people boycotted so many of the new brutality movies. Nobody had fully realized that juvenile audiences are so large and that violence is so profitable. In California the police had to station a special traffic detail at North Bedford Drive in Beverly Hills because the many psychoanalysts there were swamped with movie executives and others of the industry who were losing money on account of the delinquency strike and wanted their nerves quieted.

Firms and experts specializing in supplying communities with advice about juvenile delinquency had to go out of business. Manufacturers of phony medicines and contraptions advertised in comics and juvenile magazines lost their whole child clientèle. These advertisements had been frightening children for many years, inveigling them into spending considerable sums of money. Adults, parents, women's clubs, the Board of Health, physicians—all had been unable to stop this abuse. But post-adolescents told adolescents, and they in turn told the younger children, that they were just being gypped. So the sales and the advertising stopped.

Magazines had a hard time, too. Articles on juvenile delinquency had been sure-fire. Just when the strike got under way one national magazine had scheduled two perfect articles by two well-known authors. One was entitled:

My Child Is Delinquent

The other, scheduled for a few months later, was

My Child Is Not Delinquent

Of course both articles had to be dropped because they were no longer of any interest to readers. Circulation was also affected, along with the schedules of articles. Newspapers lost one of their best subjects for circulation drives. Juvenile delinquency had been front-page news and the subject for long feature articles. One big newspaper had started a campaign right after Santana's arrest, with a "PARENTS' PLEDGE" and photograph of the Mayor on the front page in a big boxed space. Such a campaign did not do the children any good, of course, but it was good for the newspaper. With the delinquency strike in full swing, they had to think up new devices to hike circulation. So the papers lost money. The comic-book publishers

(since children had completely stopped buying
comic books), paced up and down and debated the
possibility of founding a new Association and making
a new Code and a new Seal, as well as the problem of
locating someone to defend all three.

The income of all the experts on juvenile delinquency
was seriously curtailed. Many even had to look for
new jobs! It was particularly painful since so many
new avenues for well-paid jobs in the delinquency
field were just opening up. Before the strike everything had been going so well! There were more and
more conferences, more committees, more commis-
sions, more boards, more meetings with paid speakers,
more supervisors, more salaries, more jobs, more panel
discussions in conspicuous TV spots. Now all that was
useless. (Not that it had been useful before!) All kinds
of people whose positions depended in some way on
juvenile delinquency became unemployed. The public agencies didn't get any more appropriations and
the private agencies couldn't collect any more
money. Worst of all, schools had trouble getting
salaries for new teachers and other positions (needed
more than ever because now the schools were full of
eager pupils) because they couldn't use juvenile delinquency as an argument for bigger budgets.

Political patronage got all tangled up because all
kinds of positions, from Children's Court judges
downward, could not be given out any longer to un-
trained people who had made names for themselves
by combatting juvenile delinquency on radio and television. A real blow came when a smart trader on the
Stock Exchange noticed on his ticker tape that some

stocks having to do with pulp paper were going down sharply. He thought others would follow and sold out. That spread and caused a crisis in the investment market.

For the children, however, the strike was a great success. They stopped committing delinquent acts. They didn't have to go to reformatories any more, or to jails, or to the electric chair. They didn't even get called "hoodlums" any longer.

For the adults the strike caused trouble and embarrassment. Just when combatting juvenile delinquency was in full swing, the delinquency had stopped! It was against all theory and interfered with practice, both public and private.

The experts did not fail to draw attention to the extreme danger of the situation. As one of them pointed out, what would become of all the "pent-up aggressions" of children which now were not being "released"? Another, in an article in a Sunday newspaper, explained that the strike was nothing but an expression of the children's unconscious hostility; it was all really the fault of their mothers. And the American Civil Liberties Union issued a stern warning that the children's boycott and strike interfered with the constitutional guarantees of freedom of expression and in fact constituted "economic censorship."

It all got so disturbing that prior to election the Chairman of the Republican (or was it the Democratic?) National Committee took notice. In a television interview on the To-Day program he told Dave Garroway and the nation that they were proposing a

White House Conference on "The Peaceful Uses of
Childrens' Energy."

But the climax came soon enough. The children
realized that they had to keep up the work of perpetuating their delinquency stoppage. One afternoon
they formed a procession and paraded through Central Park. It was all very orderly. Some of the time
they sang marching songs as they went along. Dotted
here and there through the ranks of children were
large banners. They had interesting slogans:

DOWN WITH DELINQUENCY

WE WANT TO LEARN TO READ

BOOKS NOT COMIC BOOKS

DOWN WITH TRUANCY

NO MORE REFORMATORIES

DELINQUENTS ARE UNFAIR TO OTHER CHILDREN

RUDOLF FLESCH FOR MAYOR

Toward the end of the procession two groups carried
some particularly large and alarming streamers. One
read:

WE ARE ALL BROTHERS

(to which someone had added a pencil scrawl:

AND SISTERS

The other was even worse. It stated in big letters:

THERE ARE NO ENGLISH, NO SPANISH, NO NEGROES,
NO PUERTO RICANS. THERE ARE ONLY PEOPLE!

It was really outrageous. Fortunately one of the Civic Leaders well-known for combatting Juvenile Delinquency was just then passing through the park in his chauffeur-driven limousine. He was coming from one of the underprivileged segregated neighborhoods where he had been asking kids questions—from his comfortable seat in the big car. Haroun al Rashid visiting the poor!* He lost no time in reporting these goings-on to the police. Within a few minutes five police-patrol radio cars were at the scene to break up the disgraceful demonstration. In the process a few boys resisted officers. That caused a mélee and twenty children were rounded up and arrested. They were charged with unlawful assembly (they did not know you had to get permission to have a parade), assault and juvenile delinquency, and were held by the authorities.

* *This* is not fantasy: high officials did exactly this, recently —and some of the questions were about world conditions. This, incidentally, led to some misunderstandings, too, because the kids thought the "Swiss" were a rival gang and denied fighting them.

News of the events in the Park spread quickly over the country. A boy in Baltimore snatched a purse. Three juveniles in San Francisco burglarized a store. In Chicago windows were broken in a school. In the Bronx in New York one evening a shot rang out and a young boy lay dead on the pavement.

The strike was over. Order had been restored.

IX   *Guilty Justice*

"Are you talking about the new Jerusalem? says the Citizen.

"I'm talking about injustice, says Bloom."

—James Joyce: *Ulysses*

It was my task to relate Santana's mental condition to what he had done. The law makes a sharp distinction between different kinds of homicide. Murder in the first degree is punishable by death. It is considered first degree when it is committed from a deliberate and premeditated design to affect the death of the person killed or if, without a premeditated design, it is "evincing a depraved mind."

Murder in the second degree is committed with the design to affect the death of a person but without deliberation or premeditation. Manslaughter in the first degree is the killing of a human being without the design to affect death by a person engaged in committing a misdemeanor or in the heat of passion. Manslaughter in the second degree exists if the killing occurs while the person commits a trespass or in the heat of passion, but not with a dangerous weapon.

The law also recognizes what it calls justifiable homicide. That exists when there is reasonable ground to apprehend a design on the part of the person slain to commit a felony, or to do some great personal injury to the person and there is imminent danger of such design being accomplished.

This was the legal-psychological labyrinth in which the jury had to find its way. Certainly a psychiatrist should be able to be of some help to them. If a judge interprets the rules of evidence liberally, a psychiatrist can review the life of the defendant and his state of mind in great detail. But where are you when you get through? According to the criminal law you face the question: Was the defendant legally sane or insane?

It is not accidental that psychiatric testimony is so contested and so hedged around by restrictions, for it is not a side issue. It goes to the heart of the law, the question of guilt or lack of guilt. In order to premeditate, a man must have criminal intent—what the lawyers call *mens rea*. He must have a purpose or plan to harm a particular person. According to the legal idea the act itself will show the intent. Every man is liable for the natural consequences of his acts. If he is not able to form real criminal intent, he must be incompetent or insane. According to the law, if there is no criminal intent, there is no guilt. There is no middle way. A man is either 100 per cent guilty or not. He cannot be 90 per cent guilty.

If a psychiatrist cannot testify that a man is legally insane his testimony can only come under the heading of extenuating circumstances, which, of course, affects the determination of the different degrees of homicide. But the judge cannot charge the jury like that. The law does not permit him to minimize the offense by referring to the state of mind of the defendant in the sense that a psychiatrist does. That is entirely in the province of the jury. The judge is confined to the definition of the degrees of homicide. The psychiatrist is confined to the categorical question to be answered with one of two conclusions: sane or insane. But the jury is not bound by the either-or conclusions of a psychiatrist. It can take all his facts into consideration and find a lesser degree of homicide. As Professor Max Radin of the University of California expresses it, "In any case of homicide the jury can bring in a verdict of guilty of any degree it chooses, it can

determine not only whether the accused is guilty, but
what punishment he shall receive, and can do so despite the careful discrimination which the judge's
charge makes between the degrees as a matter of law."
I have often found that juries do just that. They usually do not receive the benefit of psychiatry at all, or
when they do, they get it in garbled form because
there are so many interruptions, objections, excep-
tions and contradictions by opposing experts. Fundamentally they are interested in only two questions:
Why was the murder committed and could it have
been prevented? This healthy interest is apt to get
buried in the sand of psychiatric and legal technical-
ities. I hoped to appeal to the good sense of the jury,
for I was convinced that according to the spirit of the
law neither first- nor second-degree homicide fitted
the real merits of this case.

I knew there was something wrong with Santana,
but the law can take this into account only in its own
way. Psychiatry knows gradations. But the law uses
legal insanity as a working term. It does not recognize
diminished responsibility. In some countries there is
such a law; in Scotland, for example. Dr. David Henderson in his "Reflections on Criminal Conduct and
Its Treatment" quotes Lord Alness: "Formerly there
were only two classes of prisoner—those who were
completely responsible and those who were completely irresponsible. Our law has now come to recognize in murder cases a third class—those who, while
they do not merit the description of being insane, are
nevertheless in such a condition as to reduce their
act of murder to culpable homicide. . . . There must

be a weakness or aberration of mind; there must be some form of unsoundness; there must be a mind so affected that responsibility is diminished from all responsibility to partial responsibility; the prisoner in question must only be partially responsible for his action."

Many years ago when I was the psychiatric resident at Johns Hopkins Hospital (as Dr. Henderson had been years before me) the father of a schizophrenic girl being treated in the hospital came to see me. He said he wanted to ask me only one question: "Has my daughter lost her mind or is she just a little crazy in the head?" I knew exactly what he meant, and was able to satisfy him. Although the law here does not recognize the term *diminished responsibility*, the jury is permitted to use just this train of thought when it distinguishes between different degrees.

There are no hard and fast rules for the evaluation of schizoid psychopathic personalities with regard to medico-legal evaluation. As a matter of fact, two of the most experienced psychiatrists disagree on that theoretically. The late Dr. Norwood East classified the schizoids among "the mentally inefficient" but in the generally normal group. Dr. David Henderson, on the other hand, in "Society and Criminal Conduct" stresses their abnormality and their need of special penal treatment.

There are three time periods in Santana's unlawful behavior. The first began with his acquiring of a gun; the second with his walking with Superman while Superman carried and threatened Blankenship with the gun; the third, lasting not more than a minute, when the gun went off. It is, of course, the third period which was legally the important one. The question is whether he was legally in a state of mind to use all his emotional-intellectual resources of self-control and whether the connections between the different parts of his personality were intact enough for his whole personality to function according to its best potentialities. My impression was that the connections were not functioning and that this was a short-circuit reaction. The time factor here is of the greatest importance. Supposing the crime had been counterfeiting, which takes a considerable time to plan, prepare and execute. The time would have been too long to assume such an elementary pathological reaction. There also would be absent so powerful an emotion as fear, which Santana had had since he was threatened with bodily harm the previous Thursday. What occurred, negligently or voluntarily, was an impulsive "aggressive" act such as occurs sometimes in persons who habitually show just the opposite, namely a markedly passive mental make-up.

The test for legal responsibility or sanity is knowledge of the nature and quality of the act and of the difference between right and wrong with regard to that act. This rule has been clearly related by Judge Cardozo to "the mental health and the true capacity of the criminal." The prosecution, that is to say the state, presumes that the accused is sane. Its requirements for this assumption are extremely modest. The opposite must be introduced and proved by the defense.

It is the second part of the legal definition of insanity,* the knowledge of right and wrong, that was most pertinent in my examination of Santana. Lawyers, of course, do not ask the psychiatrist whether a man knows right from wrong. They can determine that for themselves. They want to know whether the knowledge of right and wrong was lacking on account of mental disease. In other words, what the psychiatrist is really asked is whether a defendant has the *capacity* to know right from wrong and, even further afield, whether the suppositions and conditions existed for him to have the capacity to know right from wrong. We have to deduce the answer clinically.

If one were to take the criminal law literally, it assumes that ethical behavior consists in something which usually does not correspond to reality. It assumes that there is an abstract knowledge of right and wrong, that a person acts accordingly and that he either chooses the right, in which case he is good (not guilty), or he chooses the wrong, in which case he is bad (guilty). In reality we deal with a living human being, with all his contradictions, whose ethical behavior is not a schematic abstraction but a dynamic interplay of often-conflicting tendencies. Only a small

---

* The legal definition of insanity is under heavy attack. It has however helped democratic justice for many years and so far no better test has been devised. This is true of the definition recently put forward by the Court of Appeals of the District of Washington in the Durham case. (*Cf.* Wertham: "Psychoauthoritarianism and the Law." *Univ. Chicago Law Review,* Winter. 1955, pp. 336 & 569.)

part of this can be expressed in terms of knowledge and will power. Freud taught us that a man may feel guilty unconsciously. He may not "know" that he has acted wrongly, and yet he may be much stricter with himself than the law would be if his offense were known. Such a person may revert to ancient and barbaric law when he later inflicts punishments upon himself. I remember a patient at Hopkins Hospital who used an unguarded moment to blind himself by putting a needle into one eye.

One aspect of morality consists in the knowledge that actions have consequences. But that is not enough. An individual lives in a social environment which conditions him quite apart from his subjective moral reflections. This objective situation has great force. It is the basis (more or less unconscious) of his whole moral orientation.

An individual may not differentiate correctly between right and wrong because he may not even be aware at the time that the situation poses an ethical problem. On the other hand, he may think in ethical terms when he is the victim of totally different forces. Commenting on his laboratory dogs, who developed a real disturbance in behavior on account of overstimulation, Pavlov said that if it were possible to ask the dogs afterwards, they would report that they were "unable to refrain from doing that which was forbidden, and then felt punished for doing it." This is of course a laboratory situation with an animal, but it has analogies in human life.

Genuine and spontaneous regret after an action may be an indication of a realistic knowledge of right and wrong. But often what expressions of regret indicate is not the presence of developed morality but merely knowledge of the existence of a taboo. Or a person may say the "right" things purely out of fear, as the Reverend Kumado's son did in jail in Alan Paton's *Cry, the Beloved Country*. Santana's attitude was the same as if he had made a mistake in arithmetic and now knew better.

Did he know right from wrong? Did he know it as well as you would want your own brother or son or neighbor to know it? Contrary to the knowledge that two and two add up to four, which can be directly ascertained by a simple question, knowledge of right and wrong is a reaction of the whole personality, and has to be inferred.

It seemed to me that Santana suffered from ethical confusion, that he was morally mixed up. I planned to quote to the jury his own words in that respect, in their inarticulate articulateness. I asked him about stealing. He told me that he had never stolen anything. I believed him, and asked why he had never done so. His immediate reply was, "I always got money." Later, when I came back to the same question, he gave me this sample of his lack of moral judgment, "I never steal anything. I need nothing from nobody."

He seemed to have no conception of the seriousness of what he had done. When at different times I asked him whether he felt sorry, he gave a number of different replies. They speak for themselves as indicating the measure of his values of right and wrong:

"I am sorry because I did not mean to kill the guy."

"I am sorry because he want (sic) to be living like me."

"I am sorry because I did not know the guy."

"I feel sorry for my mother. She want me to be outside with her."

"I am sorry for my brothers because I am the biggest in the home."

He also told me, "I am not afraid. The only thing I am worried about is my mother—my mother and my brothers."

On the other hand, he said to me once, referring to his predicament, "I do nothing wrong—only to myself." And when I asked him at another time what sort of things made him angry he replied, "I don't get angry with people, only angry with myself. I can't explain that." He told me that the other inmates in jail had talked to him about the electric chair. I got the impression that even in jail, facing the severest punishment, he did not know what was wrong and how he could have acted otherwise. I asked him what he could have done differently to prevent what happened.

"Nothing," he answered. "They was looking for me. The Golden Guineas. What could I do?"

"What would they have done?"

"That's up to them. Beat me up or something."

It was clear that he had one principle of orientation: violence, the threat of violence and the fear of violence. He had a gun because it appeared to him that he needed one, that a gun was what one was supposed to have. What else *could* one have? He did not know of a better solution.

Discrimination between right and wrong is not merely a logical operation. It implies an emotional dynamic relationship between the individual and his surroundings. A boy like Santana may have the wherewithal for a sound sense of right and wrong which may be thwarted and deformed by the times. Ethical behavior presupposes a social orientation. In Puerto Rico the races got along with one another. The teacher he liked most was Spanish. The teachers talked about race. He had to take up Spanish because he was Puerto Rican. The racial composition of his class was impressed upon his mind. There were racial fights and near-race riots in school. He heard teachers and others say, "You don't belong here"; "You don't have that in Puerto Rico"; etc.

He was preoccupied with the whole question. "In high school," he told me, "I asked a teacher, 'Why do you always say Puerto Ricans? How do you know that I'm a Puerto Rican? Why don't you say something like Cuban or Mexican?' She didn't say nothing." In Puerto Rico things had been different: "In Puerto Rico everybody get along. The white and colored don't fight." Ethical thinking is social thinking. To a boy like Santana society, the State itself, appears unsocial.

Although he would not have expressed it so, it became clear to me that for him there were four types of people in the world:

  I. *Authority figures* such as the teacher, the truant officer, the priest, the policeman, the doctor. He does not discriminate much between them. They all have in common that they are impersonal and demanding. They want him to go to school, to church, to answer questions, take tests. They are more apt to tell him not what to do, but what not to do.

II. *The admirable, powerful people.* Of these he knows only Superman. They are on top. They can't be hurt. They can do whatever they want. They are above the authority figures, as Superman is above the police.

III. *The majority of people.* The only criterion he knows to differentiate between them is race and nationality. They are either English or Spanish or so on.

IV. *Those who are weak or inferior and unwanted.* He belongs to that group. So does his mother. So do most Puerto Ricans in general, especially those not born here, and his prison mates.

He told me he never went to confession. I asked him why he didn't talk to the priest about his troubles. He said, "He didn't ask me. If I go to the priest I tell him less because you don't remember all at the same time. But here you do." He talked to me about his confession to the police, which apparently was elaborate. He said, "It is different from telling to a priest, because to the priest you tell the truth and to the police sometimes you lie." He told me proudly, "Right in here I go to church every Sunday. I pray every night. I got books."

I had occasion to talk to the priest, whose name he had especially given me as someone who knows him. This priest was concerned about the boy. He gave me permission to quote him. He remembered Santana as being very quiet. He knew him from the High School Religious Instruction Class. These classes were large and he received no individual instruction. There had been some trouble with two different instructors who felt the boy showed no interest, that it was almost impossible to teach him. He had not been to communion since coming to this country. "He is not ignorant, he is mixed up and completely uninformed." I told the priest that it seemed to me he didn't know the difference between a confession to a priest and a confession to the police. He said that was true. He mentioned the name of another priest who knew the boy, and I talked to him, too. He also gave me permission to quote him. He said that the boy "does not realize the gravity of his crime even now. The only reason he is sorry is because he had never seen this boy. He said when he gets out of this he will stick to boxing! He can't differentiate properly between right and wrong. He has a certain amount of intelligence for retaining things. I don't think the kid can be consistent. If you come back in a week he'd give you a different answer."

I prepared to tell the jury that the boy, although not legally insane, was a mentally abnormal boy who had a disturbed sense of right and wrong. At the very least, I felt, the psychiatric testimony would supply a rational background for clemency and an incentive for measures of rehabilitation. In the courtroom of course I would have to express this in the briefest possible way. But for myself I kept in mind the fuller picture. Whether a person knows the difference between right and wrong depends on what he is. A case is not only a clinical type; he is also a unique individuality. Those who claim to study only this unique individuality tend to be unscientific. And those who want to study only the diagnostic type tend to be inhuman. The two must be combined; that is the art and the science of psychiatry.

Santana is not a criminal who lashes back at life. Hostility, anger or resentment are notably absent from his whole make-up. He is a mixture between lack of interest, compliance, withdrawal, chronic discouragement, self-effacement, docility, lack of initiative and immature impulsiveness. What was he trying to do? He was *trying to conform*. Essentially he is not a rebel but a conformist—a confused conformist. That seemed to me to be one of the keys to the whole case. He wanted to adapt himself and be regular, do what the others do and be appreciated, but still remain unnoticed. But as a boy without a father, member of a hard-pressed family and especially as a Puerto Rican in a ruthlessly hostile environment, he could not orient himself. We have heard a lot for years about displaced persons. That is not at all what Santana was. He belongs to that large group of people who do not have the opportunity or capacity to place themselves. He belongs to that category which I call the *unplaced.* Although not given serious consideration, they are a psychological and social reality.

The law assumes not only that a person is thoroughly sane, but that the society in which the crime occurs is thoroughly well ordered. Santana needed support and help. What help did society give him? Bishop Buddy of San Diego said recently, "Let's face the facts. We have failed to indoctrinate youth in the fundamentals of right and wrong. . . . Their consciences have not been trained." Whatever the remedy may be, this diagnosis is certainly correct. Judge Kaplan, chairman of the New York Youth Board, says of his experiences with children in his court: "Many seem never to have been taught the difference between right and wrong." This is not merely a question of *delinquent* children. The cynicism that we teach non-delinquent children is even worse. It derives not only from the conduct of adults but also from the demoralizing material supplied to children by the mass media. It is fashionable to say glibly that it is all up to the home. That means being completely blind to the social evils that exist outside the family, exerting pressure on it. Mrs. Santana tried hard to give her boy moral instruction and discipline. But she herself was an unplaced person who did not understand the nature of the conflicts existing right in her block.

Some people do the wrong thing because they are not sufficiently motivated to do the right thing. Santana's interests have not been developed. He is not interested in anything. That is one reason why he is not cheerful. He does not assert himself. Lacking a fixed point from which to look at himself or at the world, and lacking a social goal, he is at the mercy of changing external circumstances. Thorstein Veblen has pointed out that one human need is "social confirmation." That was denied Santana except when he excelled in boxing (for which he is not really gifted) or worked in a gang with Superman. We cannot say to him, "Here is a fine society which welcomes you, means the best for you and gives you help and encouragement. Why don't you work with us?" Surely the authorities showed an extraordinary indifference with regard to this boy. With all the money spent,* they did not care much whether he was truant or not, they did not give him vocational guidance, they let him pick up his notions of right and wrong from movies, comic books and the street. No social agency paid any attention to him. The first time any social agency took any notice of him was ten days *after the crime.*

Sitting with him in the little room in the jail I asked myself what opportunities and facilities we put at his disposal; what could he have done after that Thursday when he was threatened with bodily injury? Supposing he had gone to a police station and reported the threat. I know such cases. They would not have listened to him; if they had, they would have laughed or brushed it off. But even if a kindhearted policeman wanted to help him, he couldn't have. He could not tell any teacher or guidance person about the threat because they had not shown any personal

---

* According to official sources 23 million dollars are earmarked every year by New York City for tax-supported activities relating to juvenile delinquency.

interest in him. He couldn't tell it to the truant officer
because that would have gotten him into trouble on
account of his truancy—and the truant officer himself
would have been powerless anyhow.

Suppose he had applied to a mental hygiene clinic.
For that he needed the referral of authorities. But
even had that been possible, he would have had to
wait many months before a social worker would have
seen him—and told him that the clinic could do
nothing for him in this matter.

He couldn't tell his mother because she was as help-
less as he was and it would only have worried her.
He could have hung around at a street corner for
weeks or months until he encountered one of the street
club workers; but talking to him about the gangs
would have meant squealing on his own gang and
members of other gangs, and would not in any case
have led him to anyone in authority who would keep
his secret and have the power to protect him.

What society did give him via its mass media was a
stream of images of violence as the solution for all
problems. J. B. Priestley has said of "this new violence with its sadistic overtones" that "any lad who
tries to forget his various frustrations by continuously reading such stuff is in danger of real corruption."
Santana resisted real corruption; but it is true of him,
as George H. Pumphrey says, that "One thing is certain: children fed on a regular diet of horrors and
brutal crimes will gradually lose their sense of what is
right and wrong."

Sometimes in court a defense lawyer will say that
his client is not really guilty, that it is all the fault of

society. The prosecutor will answer with equal conviction that it is the other way round. This clash of opinion occurs also in theoretical literature on crime.
But individual guilt and social responsibility do not
exclude each other mechanically. The fact that society is ultimately responsible for a crime does not
completely relieve the individual of guilt. Nor does the
fact that the individual is guilty relieve society of all
responsibility. There is a dynamic interconnection between them.* What Santana saw around him was
that might is right. Like most people who don't have
might and who cannot qualify as supermen, he looked
for a system of right. What he was taught at home was
totally different from what he saw in school or on the
street, or in comic books and movies. So he looked for
might again. He borrowed a Beretta.

Santana was to have his day in court. By that time
I was convinced that I wanted to do everything to
protect him from extreme punishment, and perhaps
even get him somewhere where at least an attempt
could be made at rehabilitation.

Up to the very last moment Santana had the hiss
of the papers and newscasters against him. When
the trial got under way they gave again "the univer-
sally accepted version" and spoke about "Santana's
mob" and of the victim as "the model student who
had never belonged to any gang." They kept on

---

* The paradox is that when in the distant future we have
created an ideal society, in which the individual will be
solely and wholly responsible for his transgressions, he will
not wish to commit any (unless he is seriously diseased).

speaking of "Frank Tarzan Santana" or "Tarzan Santana." They described him as "stolid," "cowed and sullen" looking, having a "sullen scowl on his face," sitting "as if he were thoroughly disinterested"—a "study in nonchalance!"

The district attorney knew, of course, that we (the lawyers and I) had the true facts about the circumstances. For the public the trial started with some wrangling about whether Puerto Ricans are ever on special juries like that trying Santana. Meanwhile, paradoxically through the devoted Maria, contact behind the scenes was established between prosecution and defense, and a plea for second-degree murder was agreed upon. That usually means imprisonment for from twenty years to life.

The average man believes that all, or at least a majority of persons charged with a felony, have a jury trial. Nothing could be further from the truth. Only a small minority get the chance to face a jury. When a lesser plea is recommended and accepted, the jury does not hear the evidence and the case is decided administratively. So Santana did *not* have his day in court.

The district attorney played his cards close to his chest. As I understand it, the district attorney represents *all* the people of his district, including the accused. By giving no hint to the press that the version which for almost two months had so inflamed public opinion was false, he had helped to unleash forces which he now had to face. He was like the Sorcerer's Apprentice. So he approached the victim's father and Mr. Blankenship addressed the court, endorsing the plea. Well-meant as this speech was on the father's part, it was unnecessary except to save face for the district attorney. For there was no case for a first-degree murder charge. The assistant district attorney (who prosecuted the case) told the court, "I have serious doubts that any jury would return a first-degree verdict." And he told Mr. Blankenship, who later told the press, "That on a charge of first-degree murder the boy would probably get off with a *Not Guilty* verdict."

As to the facts themselves, the district attorney told the court and said in interviews to the press and on television afterwards that young Blankenship had belonged to a gang, that he (*not* Santana) had been the aggressor and did the pushing, that there had been *no* previous offenses by Santana (some newspapers had reported that there were some, and this had not been corrected). He further stated in these public interviews that *Blankenship* had tried to induce other members of his school to join his gang, and that he "had a chip on his shoulder" and "had gone a long distance from home that day spoiling for a fight." The district attorney himself now characterized the way the case had been reported by "press, radio and television" as "irresponsible." While Santana got the gun originally, Superman and other boys got it and loaded it. According to the district attorney, up to the time that Blankenship pushed one of the boys "Santana played no part." The district attorney knew many other details, including the fact that Santana had been "set upon" and threatened two days before.

The effect of all this was not a better understanding of Santana's life and situation, but an attack on the victim, who was dead. The district attorney even dragged in the fact that Blankenship "had a record of bad conduct in grammar school"! Different papers reported in identical words that he "blasted" the reputation of the slain boy. One paper had a blazing headline that

Victim Is Called Hoodlum

and the story stated that "Blankenship was pictured by the state as a hoodlum who roamed the streets spoiling for a fight."

So the community's reaction had made a full circle—a vicious circle. First a lynch spirit had been aroused with a uniformity that affected all the media of communication. Then, when this lynch spirit had been frustrated, the residual abuse was heaped on the victim. This vicious circle is typical of the community's attitude in general to the current violence in juvenile delinquency.

Santana's pleading guilty to a second-degree murder charge was purely a legal fiction. He certainly did not understand what such a plea really implied. He was obliging and conforming to the very last. Called to stand before the Court, he spoke in his usual low voice. Admonished by the Court to speak louder, he said, "Yes, sir. Yes, sir."

Young Bill Blankenship was a bright, good-looking, sociable and decent boy. By any standards of prediction he would have made something of his life and been a pride to his family. He was a victim in a triple sense. His life was cut short just as he was growing up.

He did not invent juvenile gangs; but like so many other youngsters he was sucked into their whirlpool. What was the last gang battle about? Just before the last sidewalk encounter he asked some of his friends to join in the fight against the "Puerto Ricans." He had not invented this antagonism, either, and he would never have had it if he had not lived in a community seething with it. He was a victim in a third sense. After his death his failings were magnified and broadcast.

What in the last analysis caused Billy Blankenship's tragedy? As in any such case, there is a *constellation of factors*. And one factor may be reduced to another. But we must arrive at a balance somewhere and have the courage to draw conclusions. The background of that fatal sidewalk encounter included many boys. Each of them had an outer and an inner life history. They all had families and were exposed to many influences from the street, from mass media, from adults, in school and in social life. There is not just one single characteristic that distinguishes a delinquent from a non-delinquent. A little more or a little less of any factor may make an enormous difference. The balance between happiness and unhappiness, between health and disease, between crime and non-crime, and in this case between life and death, may rest on that.

From this larger perspective we can see what set these children against each other and led them to find such outlets. The adult community's attitude against Puerto Ricans was the most potent, the most traumatic factor in Santana's dislocation. As reflected in his mind, it affected all the common relationships of his life. What would be the best method to confuse a boy? Ask him to adjust to a society and at the same time make him feel that he is not really part of it. As the director of the University of Maryland's Institute for Child Study put it, "Among children there is nothing as likely to make them delinquent as the realization that they are regarded as second-rate citizens." (I would qualify that by saying that it makes them *prone* to delinquency.) In Santana's case, there was added a sense of personal inadequacy and the effect of mass indoctrination with violence.

Inversely, this feeling against Puerto Ricans affected young Blankenship as well. Neither boy learned race prejudice in his home. It came from outside. Where there is so much hostility in the environment, it would mean looking through the wrong end of the telescope to stress the hostility of the individual child. It was on the altar of community prejudice and antagonism that Billy Blankenship was sacrificed.

Sentence was pronounced on July fifteenth. With a plea taken, there is of course no trial. Since the law fixes the minimum sentence at twenty years to life, the judge could not go below that. He did not try to. He gave him an even harsher sentence. As one paper put it, he threw the book at him: twenty-five years to life.

Newspapers and radio reports played again the same old record. They still called Santana "Tarzan." Big headlines announced:

TARZAN GIVEN 25 YEARS TO LIFE

They still called him a "hoodlum," too. They did not fail to mention that he was "swarthy" (thus calling attention to his nationality), said he was "hotheaded" and of "low intelligence." Some repeated that he was being sentenced "for the senseless gangland execution" and told again the old story of *his* having been "on the prowl looking for vengeance" and having "wrongly suspected Blankenship of being in the enemy camp." As Fern Marya of the New York *Post* put it: "New York had manufactured a fantasy."

One Spanish-language paper correctly reported that in court he showed himself very serious and attentive (*"Muy serio y atento"*). But the others said again that he "appeared unemotional," "showed no sign of emotion," "listened almost indifferently" and "appeared bored."

He is now in a jail about 250 miles from New York, which makes it very difficult for his family to visit him. He wants to get his high-school diploma by studying in prison. He also works in the carpenter shop, for which he gets five cents (5¢) a day. He has figured out —wrongly—that in this way he can save thousands of dollars. He is considered "a model prisoner."

When Santana was led away from the almost empty courtroom the case was settled. But how can a community handle the violence in its midst if it doesn't learn the true story? The public heard of one hoodlum, then of another. One was dead, the other disposed of. In connection with this fatal sidewalk encounter fourteen boys had been seized on various charges. I have seen sworn statements of eyewitnesses according to which it is not even excluded that Santana's gun went off *accidentally* when he grabbed it!

What did society want? Did it want revenge? Did it want just to eliminate the culprit? Did it want to rehabilitate him? Did it want to deter others? Did it want to fight juvenile delinquency? As it was, the community could learn nothing from this case—not how to protect itself nor how to protect its children.

Whatever the individuals themselves thought subjectively, there was a social motive why the community did not want a trial. If it had looked into this boy's mind, it would have had to look at itself. He was not the only confused conformist. If the community looked at the whole situation of Santana and of the fourteen boys seized in connection with the case, it would have had to look in a mirror. Some mirrors, as everyone knows, give an unflattering picture, showing the rings under the eyes and unwanted wrinkles. Pascal described man as a being who cannot know himself without wishing that he were different (*sans se vouloir autre*). That is true of society, too. It was easier to send the boy away without a trial and let things be as they are.

I had occasion to speak about the case with one of my ex-delinquent adolescents who had made a very good adjustment. I asked him what he thought about the sentence. "That means," he said, "that he has to stay in jail at least almost twenty years. He might as well stay there for good! I'd rather stay there. I'd go out and rob something—anything to get back. When he gets out what can he do? They won't give him a job. They'll ask him: 'Where have you been all these years? In the slammer [jail]?' He could not get a job, except hustling—selling sticks [marijuana]."

Is that the lesson society wants to teach? What this boy said is the kind of reaction that decided me— since I could not testify to my findings in court—to write them for a larger jury.

Index